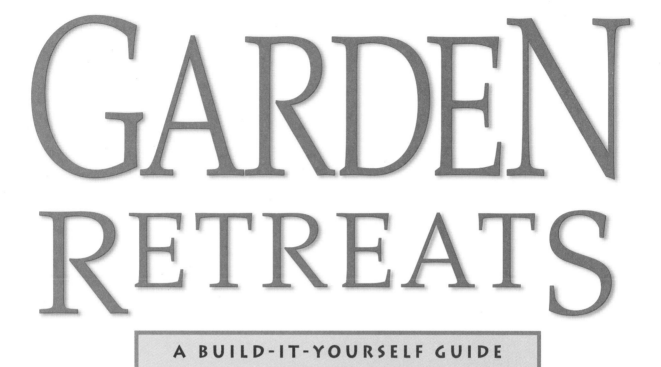

GARDEN RETREATS

A BUILD-IT-YOURSELF GUIDE

David & Jeanie Stiles

Illustrations by David Stiles

STOREY
BOOKS

The mission of Storey Communications is to serve our customers by publishing practical information that encourages personal independence in harmony with the environment.

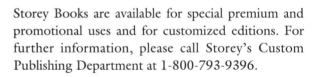

Dedication

To Tillybrack Cottage, in Monymusk, Scotland — at the foot of Benachie Hill, surrounded by heather and hollyhocks.

Edited by Janet Lape and Dan Callahan
Cover design by Rob Johnson, Johnson Design
Front and back cover photographs by David Stiles
Text design by Mark Tomasi
Text production by Erin Lincourt
Line drawings by David Stiles
Indexed by Hagerty & Holloway

Storey Books are available for special premium and promotional uses and for customized editions. For further information, please call Storey's Custom Publishing Department at 1-800-793-9396.

Printed in Canada by Transcontinental Printing
10 9 8 7 6 5 4 3 2 1

Library of Congress Cataloging-in-Publication Data

Stiles, David R.
    Garden Retreats : a build-it-yourself guide / [by David and Jeanie Stiles] ; drawings by David Stiles.
        p. cm.
    Includes bibliographical references and index.
    ISBN 1-58017-149-4 (alk. paper)
    1. Garden structures—Design and construction— Amateurs' manuals. I. Stiles, Jeanie, 1944- .
    II. Title
TH4961.S754 1999
684. 1'8—dc21   98-55328
                                                     CIP

Contents

Acknowledgements

Many thanks to Helena Cresci, whose pergola graces our cover, and to her magnificent garden, which enhances its uniqueness. We also wish to thank Janet Lape, Dan Callahan, and Bob Moran, whose enthusiasm and expertise helped bring this book to fruition.

Introduction

A garden retreat can be as ornate or as simple as you choose. Any place that you visualize building, whether it is in the corner of a garden or a clearing in the middle of a forest, can become a place of refuge, privacy, and seclusion. A simple covered seat or bench, placed at the end of a perennial garden, can be your personal sanctuary. A bridge built over a pond filled with water lilies and fringed with Japanese Iris can be a perfect place for meditation or reading. A rose arbor can lead to a path cut through a field of ornamental grasses. A garden retreat is a personal thing. Take these designs and adapt them to your needs and situation, and make them into a garden retreat that suits you.

Garden Retreats contains 22 designs, many of which can be built in a weekend and, in most cases, using only hand tools. The advantages of building your own garden retreat include saving money, building something to fit your particular specifications and garden environment, and the obvious satisfaction of planning and building a project yourself.

This book is written for woodworkers with an interest in gardening and for gardeners who have some carpentry skills. Each project includes a materials list and detailed shop drawings and illustrations of the finished projects. You will not only be able to understand the construction process through reading the text, but also be able to visualize how to build each project by referring to the clear, step-by-step illustrations.

One of us being a designer, the other a writer, we often approach direction giving in very different ways. The designer tends to ignore the written instructions and rely solely on the diagrams, while the writer carefully reads each step of the directions in sequence. Having acknowledged the difference in the way we perceive things, we have tried to use it to our advantage when writing this book. In other words, we have attempted to appeal to both right- and left-brain types!

Fundamentals

Important things to know before you begin.

Planning

A garden project, especially any permanent structures, like a garden house, large pergola, or pool, should be carefully thought out before it's constructed. This can either be an exciting or a frustrating experience, depending upon how you approach it. To facilitate the planning stage of your construction project and to make it a more enjoyable experience, we offer the following suggestions:

Permits — If you choose to build a structure of any significant size, be sure to check with your local area building department before beginning construction to see if you need a building permit.

Good Neighbors — If your building project will be visible to your neighbors, it is a good idea to show them a sketch of your design and get their blessing before you start construction.

Appearance — You will never know exactly how a particular design will look until you have built it. There are, however, four things you can do to help you visualize how an object will look in your garden.

1. Take a photograph of the location where the project is to be built and, using a pen with waterproof ink, sketch your design right onto the photograph. If it is difficult to visualize your project on the site, place stakes in the ground to correspond with the measurements of the project and then take your photograph. Before building the rose arbor we describe in this book, we photographed our client on the site, to give the photograph more scale.

2. If you have access to your original house plans, use them as a guide to map out where you plan to situate your garden retreat and the surrounding garden.

3. If you are even slightly artistic, make an overlay by taking a piece of clear prepared acetate and taping it over a photograph of your building site. Outline your garden design in waterproof ink and, using acrylics or opaque

watercolors, paint the proposed project onto the back of the acetate.

4. Another useful visual aid is to construct a scale model of the garden project that you are building. Draw your design to scale (1" equals 1') on cardboard, cut it out using an Exacto knife, and glue the pieces together with white glue. Three-dimensional models take very little time to make and can be extremely helpful, often pointing out potential problems. We always make models for any major building project, both for our own edification and for our client's. You can also photograph the model by having someone hold it in front of the proposed site while you look through the camera lens, making adjustments until the model is in focus and in the correct position. You'll be amazed at how true to life the project looks in the developed photo.

Wood to Use Outdoors

Redwood is probably the most well known of all the rot-resistant woods grown in the United States, and it is readily available in various dimensions in all lumber yards. It is with some misgivings that we recommend it for so many of the projects in this book, since the trees from which it comes are so magnificent! But it is hard to beat for beauty and lasting ability. We once built a deck out of spruce, which was decayed in less than five years. Unhappy with the prospect of re-doing the same job after such a short time, we invested in redwood for our second deck, carefully picking out, cutting, and nailing each expensive piece of lumber ourselves. That was in 1979; with a little spring maintenance, our deck looks like new again each summer. We sand it lightly with a palm sander to remove the dirt, and brush it with a water sealer which, after a couple of days, turns the color of the wood back into a rich shade of reddish brown. This is one annual chore we actually look forward to, since the results are so satisfying.

Pressure-treated (**P.T.**) lumber is **southern pine** that has been treated with chemicals so that it can come in contact with the ground without rotting. Because of these qualities, pressure-treated wood is a practical solution for any structure that is likely to touch the ground. When using pressure-treated wood, be aware that it frequently contains CCA (chromated copper arsenate), and make sure to take all necessary precautions. These include wearing gloves and a mask when sawing through wood, and washing all exposed areas of your skin before eating or drinking. It's also a good idea to seal the ends of pressure-treated wood with a moisture repellent, to help lock in toxic chemicals and to prolong the life of the wood. Do your sawing outdoors, and cut the wood over a plastic tarp so sawdust can be disposed of and does not leach into the ground. And never burn pressure-treated wood.

Although southern pine is beautiful in its natural state, when treated with chemicals it becomes a not-so-desirable shade of green. Some attractive stains have recently become available that are made expressly for pressure-treated lumber. Osmose makes a semi-transparent stain that makes pressure-treated wood look like teak! Another option, one we have used with great success, is to cover the wood with a gray stain, which gives it an immediate weathered look.

Some of the most rot-resistant woods grown in the United State are **cypress,** which originates along the Gulf Coast, and **black locust,** which grows in the Northeast. We found a quantity of cypress in our local lumber yard on Long Island almost 20 years ago and bought as much as we could lay our hands on. Having been over-cut, it has not been harvested much over the last decade and is difficult to find except where it is grown locally. Clear cypress has a beautiful honey-colored grain and is slightly harder than pine. We used a few pieces of cypress to build a garden bench 15 years ago, and although some lichen has grown on it, the wood is in fine shape. Cypress is so impervious to water that fallen trees that have been submerged in Florida swamps for years are pulled out and sawed up to make beautiful lumber.

Although it may take some searching, once you find a source for this wonderful wood you will be instantly pleased with the results.

Black locust has been used for hundreds of years to make posts to hold up houses. When freshly cut, it has a greenish yellow cast to it and is slightly heavier than pine. Locust is a fast-growing, long-lasting wood. We have yet to locate anyone who has milled it into lumber, probably because it is best used for posts. We once built an "Irish" garden house using locust log ends, mortared into the wall. Our supply of locust came from a wood lot 150 miles away, where we made periodic trips, loading our car as heavily as we dared with fallen locust wood. Fortunately for us, a hurricane struck that summer, near where we were building the garden house, and downed several locust trees. (Locust trees suffer from a weak root system.) Our neighbors were happy to have us remove their fallen trees, giving us more than enough wood to finish building the garden house.

Red cedar is the last on the list of weather-resistant woods. Both cedar and pressure-treated southern pine are comparable in price, but we generally choose cedar. It has an appealing color and is lightweight and easy to work with. Cedar will last longer outdoors than any of the other softwoods, but we feel its longevity is slightly overrated, based on the condition of the cedar shake roof on our barn! Other types of wood should be avoided for outdoor use unless painted, given a coat of solid stain, or oiled regularly. **Pine,** for example, is not rot-resistant, but it can be periodically coated with generous amounts of wood preservative to keep it from turning gray and to extend its life.

Only **exterior plywood,** which is made with waterproof glues to keep it from delaminating, should be used outside.

Generally, it is a good idea not to varnish or paint outdoor structures, as they begin to blister and peel after a few years and become a nuisance to maintain. Stain is a better choice, and solid stains can give the appearance of paint without the problems of peeling.

Specialty Woods

The longest lasting specialty hardwood for outdoor projects that we have discovered is **greenheart.** It is so rot- and insect-proof that it is often used to make footings in the Virgin Islands, where termites can consume an entire house in no time at all. Greenheart logs were used to build several of the New York Harbor piers 150 years ago, and they remain solid even today. It is so dense that it will immediately sink when placed in water. It has a beautiful reddish color, somewhere between mahogany and teak, and is remarkably care free; it needs only a light oiling once a year to retain its color.

There are some disadvantages to this extreme density and hardness, however. It is impossible to drive a nail into the wood, and when using screws, you must first drill an oversize pilot hole, so that the screw threads barely catch the wood. Make sure you position the screw correctly, since you will not be able to remove it once it is imbedded in the wood. Some wood shops refuse to use it, since it dulls their saws. Curiously enough, when it is cut with a saw, it gives off green sawdust, hence the name "greenheart." It is expensive and must be special-ordered from a supplier, but it is a good wood to use sparingly for a special project. We used greenheart to make a planter just outside our kitchen window, and its mellow color made a warm backdrop for the lush green herbs.

Two other specialty woods that can be ordered from a lumber yard are **Honduras mahogany** and **teak.** They are imported from South America and Indonesia, respectively. Because of their ability to withstand harsh weather, both woods are used extensively on boats. These specialty woods are expensive, but they are often worth their high costs, showing off small projects beautifully. Let the wood weather to a silvery gray, or periodically finish it off with a brightener and sealer. Teak has the added advantage of having both its own self-lubricating oil and a distinctive aroma.

Tools and Supplies

Most of the garden retreats in this book can be built using basic hand tools; however, in some cases a table saw would be useful and is a good investment if you enjoy carpentry. Here are the most useful power tools that we recommend you invest in, if you don't already own them:

Circular Saw

A portable, electric circular saw is an indispensable tool for making quick rough cuts on the site, especially if you are considering building any of the larger projects. We prefer the relatively small (6") lightweight saws that have the blade on the left side, where you can see it.

Table Saw

A 10" table saw is an essential tool for making accurate miter cuts, bevel cuts, fine cuts, and rip cuts along the length of a board. It is lightweight enough to be transported easily, yet strong enough to last a lifetime. It is not cheap, but is the workhorse of any woodshop.

Jig Saw

An electric jig saw allows you to make curved cuts, scrolls, or notches and is easy to use. Our favorite is the variable-speed Bosch jig saw.

Cordless Drill

A cordless electric drill also comes in handy. Hitachi makes a good one.

Sanders

If you have a lot of sanding to do, consider buying a palm orbital sander. It is generally considered to be a finishing sander and is used in the last stages of a carpentry project, right before painting.

If you want to shape as well as remove a lot of material, a belt sander is the best choice. It is a serious machine and must be used with caution, otherwise it can gouge your work. You can turn the belt sander upside down and use it as a table sander to smooth small pieces of wood. We have even seen carpenters sharpen chisels on a belt sander.

Rotary or disc sanders, or grinders, are strictly for heavy-duty work and are useful for sanding quantities of wood in seconds. However, these sanders will leave large swirls in the wood, which must be removed by using a belt sander with a coarse-grit sanding belt.

One of the best presents you can give yourself is a 6" × 36" table belt sander. Every time we use it, we are amazed at how effortlessly it cleans up our carpentry, leaving a clean, crisp look. It makes the difference between an average job and a highly professional looking piece of work.

Sandpaper

Sandpaper comes in 9" × 11" sheets or belts and is available in several grits, ranging from coarse to medium to fine. It is calibrated in numbers, with 24 referring to very coarse and 150 referring to extra fine. The smaller the number, the larger the grit size.

There are various types of grit, the most common being aluminum oxide, which is brown or reddish brown in color. Garnet sandpaper, which is orange in color, is also a good choice to use.

If you are sanding by hand, it is useful to make a sanding block from a scrap piece of lumber. Cover it with half a sheet of sandpaper, cut lengthwise. (An easy way to cut sandpaper is to score it on the back, fold it over a table edge, and rip it along the fold.)

To sand in tight corners, fold a full sheet of sandpaper into eighths; to sand round holes, curl a sheet of sandpaper into a tight roll. A good way to sand curved edges is shown in Rose Arbor on page 49.

Sanding is perhaps the most boring part of carpentry, but it is also the step that makes your work look the most professional. To keep this job from becoming too labor intensive, don't use only fine-grit sandpaper, but instead use a range of grits, beginning with the coarsest and graduating into the finest grit for the final smooth finish. A good selection of sandpaper to have on hand is #60 (coarse), #80 (medium), and #120 (fine).

Glues

There are only two types of glue that we recommend using on outdoor projects, and both are considered weather resistant. The first is an improved yellow glue called Titebond II. This is a one part water-resistant glue that bonds in a few minutes and should be used in areas that will be covered up with paint and not exposed to constant moisture. Use clamps to keep the pieces together while the glue dries, which takes approximately one hour if the temperature is above 55°F. It has a limited shelf life and should never be allowed to freeze.

The second (and our favorite) type of glue is West System epoxy resin, which is waterproof and consists of two parts, resin and hardener. It is expensive but well worth the price, considering how effective it is. The beauty of it is its versatility. Its consistency allows it to penetrate into the fibers of the wood, especially the end grain. It can also be mixed with a filler or a thickener, such as Micro Fiber Powder, and made into a paste to fill large gaps or dents. The drawback is that epoxy sets too fast in hot weather (10 to 15 minutes) and too slowly in cold weather (2 to 6 hours). Clamping is not always necessary for this superglue.

The epoxy is mixed in a 5-to-1 ratio with the hardener, which is difficult to do unless you buy two hand-pump dispensers, sold expressly for this purpose. One stroke of each pump is all you need for a perfect mix. We always keep a supply of 4-ounce paper cups and ¼" disposable brushes on hand for mixing epoxy glue in small quantities. Don't mix epoxy in wax-paper cups, since the heat generated by the epoxy will melt the wax, which destroys the holding power of the glue. Acetone is a good solvent to use for cleaning up your hands and any spills after gluing is completed. This glue generates its own heat, and if a large quantity is mixed in a small confined container on a hot day, it will harden up too quickly. When you need to use a lot of the glue, the perfect container is a disposable aluminum chicken pot pie plate.

The best way to get the maximum bonding power from your glue is to carefully coat both pieces with a thin layer of glue. Spread the glue with a flat stick, and keep it away from the edges so that it won't ooze out from the sides. If you are gluing the end grain of a piece of wood and it has soaked up the glue, make sure to re-coat the wood before you put the pieces together. Press the pieces of wood together and shift them slightly. You should feel the pieces pull together. When gluing joints, put pressure on the pieces by clamping them together while the glue is drying. If you don't have a large supply of clamps, you can use rope or cord, or even tape, to temporarily hold the pieces together. Clean up any spills immediately, or they may be difficult to stain later on.

Posts and Gates

The construction and installation of posts should not be taken lightly, as they are the main supporting structure for pergolas, arbors, and gates. The strength and life of the structure depends upon how well you prepare the posts.

Great care should be taken in the selection of wood. Check to make sure that the pieces you choose are free from warping. Locust is one of the best types of wood for posts, but it is seldom seen in lumberyards except as a companion for split-rail fences. As mentioned earlier, redwood and pressure-treated southern pine are the next most desirable, followed by red cedar. Although red cedar is a strong wood, it has a limited life unless steps are taken to protect it against dry rot and insects, especially termites. At the very least, the butt

▸ BUILDING TIPS

- As you cut the materials to size, label each piece on an end that won't show.

- If available, use two electric drills, so you don't have to keep changing the bits back and forth. For example, when installing screws, use a drill bit for the pilot holes and a screwdriver bit for the screws.

- When using an electric drill, use high speeds for boring wood and slower speeds for drilling holes in metal.

- For a more professional looking job, always countersink flathead screws.

- A good investment is a #6 HSS (high-speed steel) countersink drill with a stop-collar combination. This little tool drills a tapered pilot hole with a countersink hole at the top. It can be adjusted with an Allen wrench to suit your specific project.

- It is easier and more accurate to join pieces of wood by gluing them first and then screwing them together after the glue is partially dry. By using glue, the pieces tend to slip less during assembly, and the joints will be stronger. If you are going to paint your project, use auto-body filler to fill gaps quickly. It sets up hard in 10 minutes and is easy to sand.

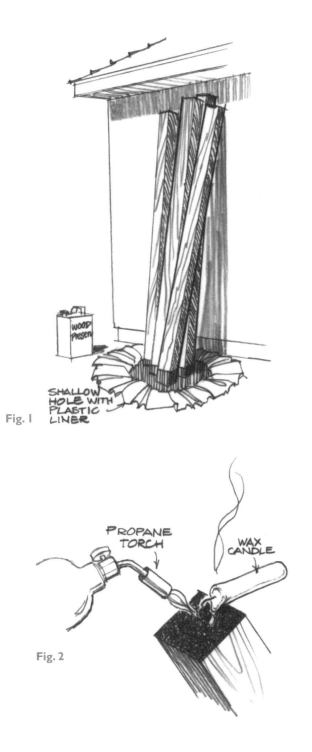

Fig. 1

SHALLOW HOLE WITH PLASTIC LINER

PROPANE TORCH

WAX CANDLE

Fig. 2

(bottom) ends of the posts should be soaked overnight in wood preservative. The easiest way of doing this is to stand the posts up in a shallow pan or a trench lined with heavy plastic sheeting (see **fig. 1**).

In colonial times, farmers would sometimes burn the ends of posts, which would provide a charcoal surface that was unsavory to bugs. To keep the post from being affected by frost heave, they would sometimes sharpen the bottom ends before burying them.

Another good way to ensure that the post you plant will outlive you is to coat the bottom end of it with wax. Place the post bottom-end up, and heat it with a propane torch. When the end grain of the wood is very hot and begins to smolder, rub a candle against it, covering it with wax. You will notice how the pores of the wood open up under heat and practically suck the wax inside. Once the wood cools, the pores close, encapsulating the wax and making the wood impervious to moisture and termites (see **fig. 2**).

The most vulnerable part of any post is directly above where it emerges from the ground, a place where wet conditions encourage deterioration and rot. To protect this area, cover the bottom end of the wood with a generous coating of roofing tar, continuing 6" above where the post emerges from the ground. We use a piece of shingle for this messy job, dabbing the tar on liberally and disposing of the shingle when we are finished (see **fig. 3**).

Posts should always be buried with a large stone or brick at the bottom of the post hole, to facilitate drainage of ground water and

Fig. 3

ROOFING TAR

make a strong foundation. Don't be too anxious to backfill the post hole immediately after the post is in place. Instead, use a temporary brace until the structure is completed, allowing you to make last minute adjustments. Nothing is more frustrating than digging up a post after you have finished burying it.

When backfilling, it is important to gradually add small amounts of soil, tamping down the area with a 2 × 4. Bear in mind that a post gets most of its strength from the friction caused by the earth pressing against its sides. Ideally, a post should have one-third of its length buried in the ground. However, if you are using a manual post-hole digger, the maximum you can bury it is about 30".

Larger posts (especially pedestals) are often built hollow and secured to a 4 × 4 pressure-treated post, pre-installed in the ground. If you are using this method, position the outer post 1" above the ground (see **fig. 4**). This will allow air to reach inside the post and keep the finished trim lumber off the damp ground.

Most posts are topped off with a wooden cap to help keep rain from entering the end grain of the wood. A typical cap is made from clear redwood and has a conical shape to help deflect water. Since this shape is difficult to make without sophisticated tools, lumberyards generally carry a line of redwood caps to fit most posts. They come in two basic styles, those that slip over the end of a post and those that are glued and nailed directly to the top of a post. Finials are another popular decorative element, and they screw easily into the post (see **figs. 5a and 5b**).

When building a gate, it is essential to have two strong posts supporting it. It is also important to understand the dynamic forces acting on the gate when it is swinging. When a gate is swung open, all the weight of the gate is pushing down and toward the bottom hinge and, at the same time, pulling away from the top hinge. To help transfer this force, it is advisable to attach a brace, extending diagonally from the top inside edge of the gate to the bottom

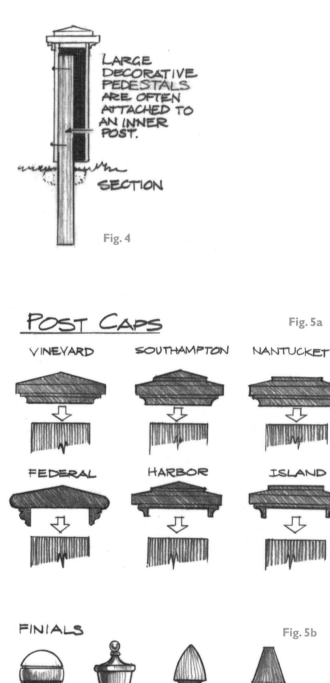

LARGE DECORATIVE PEDESTALS ARE OFTEN ATTACHED TO AN INNER POST.

SECTION

Fig. 4

POST CAPS   Fig. 5a

VINEYARD   SOUTHAMPTON   NANTUCKET

FEDERAL   HARBOR   ISLAND

FINIALS   Fig. 5b

BALL   URN   SPADE   MONUMENT

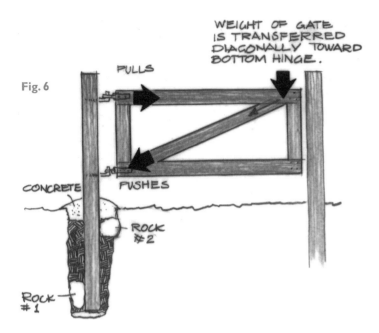

Fig. 6

WEIGHT OF GATE IS TRANSFERRED DIAGONALLY TOWARD BOTTOM HINGE.

PULLS

PUSHES

CONCRETE

ROCK #2

ROCK #1

hinge side (see **fig. 6**). When you are setting the gatepost in the ground, another way to help stabilize it is to place two rocks in the ground, one against the bottom outside edge of the post and a second one wedged against the inside of the post just below ground level (see **fig. 6**).

Although it is not generally necessary to use concrete to set fence posts, it is always a good idea to use it when setting a gatepost, in addition to wedging rocks in the sides of the post hole. Most 4 × 4 posts take a 40-pound bag of concrete mix; 6 × 6 posts, at least an 80-pound bag.

After backfilling two-thirds of the hole with soil, fill the remainder with concrete, mixed stiffly. Make a slight mound where the concrete meets the post, to shed rainwater. After a year, check to see if a gap has opened up between the concrete and the post; if it has, seal the hole with silicone caulking.

When designing your gate, be sure to make the opening wide enough to allow a wheelbarrow, lawnmower, and other garden equipment to pass through. It is often helpful to build a section of removable fencing next to the gate, as well.

Setting Corner Markers

Many of the projects in this book require some sort of markers to establish the footprint of your building project. Whether you are digging a foundation, setting concrete corner blocks, or burying posts, it is vital to mark the exact location of the corners.

Once the site has been cleared and leveled, pound four stakes into the ground, approximately where you want the structure to go. Choose one of the stakes to be the constant, that is, a point that will not change.

To make sure the corners are square, measure the diagonals. Use the Pythagorean theorem ($A^2+B^2=C^2$) to calculate the length of the diagonals, or simply adjust the corner stakes until the diagonals are of equal lengths.

Once you have established the corners of your structure, you need a way to periodically check their location, since they have to be removed to construct your foundation. In larger structures, such as houses, an elaborate system of batter boards are set up several feet away from the construction area. A much simpler method is to set two off-set stakes at each corner, and wrap mason's string around them (see **fig. 7**). Once the string is level and in place, the corner stakes can be removed and work can begin. The string can be removed from the off-set stakes when it is in the way of construction and put back whenever the exact corners need to be checked.

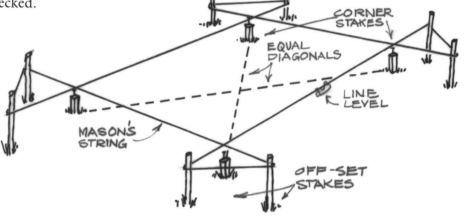

Fig. 7

Garden Seating

Every gardener needs a place to rest her weary bones.

— Mother Stiles

Abbie's Covered Seat

Patterns of light filter through the lattice of this relaxing garden seat. Constructed of clear cedar, it is both an elegant and a practical design. It could be the feature of a summer garden, covered with tendrils of evening blooming vines and English ivy, or a seat for two on a porch or patio. This garden seat is a variation of a design by Abbie Zabar, an avid herb gardener and author of garden and children's books.

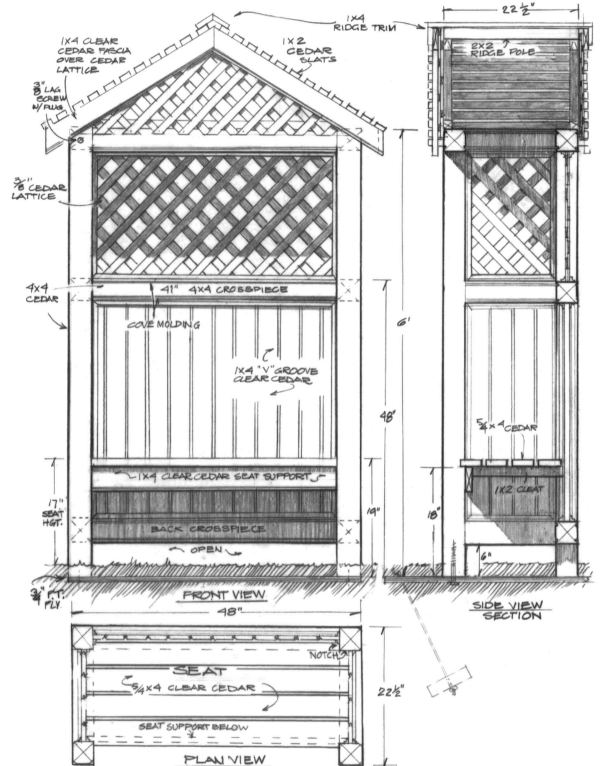

1X4 RIDGE TRIM

22½"

2X2 RIDGE POLE

1X4 CLEAR CEDAR FASCIA OVER CEDAR LATTICE

1X2 CEDAR SLATS

⅜" LAG SCREW W/PLUG

⅜" CEDAR LATTICE

4X4 CEDAR

41" 4X4 CROSSPIECE

COVE MOLDING

6'

1X4 "V" GROOVE CLEAR CEDAR

48"

5/4 X 4 CEDAR

1X4 CLEAR CEDAR SEAT SUPPORT

17" SEAT HGT.

1X2 CLEAT

18"

19"

BACK CROSSPIECE

OPEN

6"

¾" PT. PLY.

FRONT VIEW

48"

SIDE VIEW SECTION

NOTCH

SEAT

5/4X4 CLEAR CEDAR

22½"

SEAT SUPPORT BELOW

Fig. 1

PLAN VIEW

Qty.	Size	Description	Location or Use
2	12'	4 × 4 clear cedar posts	corner posts
1	8'	4 × 4 clear cedar	horizontal side pieces
2	8'	4 × 4 clear cedar	crosspieces
8	12'	1 × 4 clear cedar V-groove	lower sides and back
6	10'	1 × 2 clear cedar	slats and cleats
1	4' × 8' panel	diagonal cedar lattice	sides and back
1	4' × 4' sheet	¾" exterior plywood	base
2	6'	2 × 4 cedar	rafters
2	8'	2 × 2 cedar	purlins, crosstie, and ridgepole
3	8'	⅝ × 4 clear cedar	seat
1	10'	2 × 6 clear cedar	cove molding
2	8'	1 × 4 clear cedar	fascia
1	36"	¾"-diameter dowel	plugs
18	⅜" × 6"	lag screws	
2 lbs.	2"	galvanized finishing nails	

Wall Frame

1. Cut the two 4 × 4 cedar posts to four 6' lengths. Sand them smooth, using several grades of 60- to 120-grit sandpaper, coarse to smooth. Number the top of each post, and draw an arrow showing its relation to where the center of the structure will be (see **fig. 2**). This is an important step, since it is easy to mix up the pieces when assembling them.

2. Using a carpenter's square, mark the position where each lag screw will go, 1½" or 2" from the ends of each 6' post. Note that the holes are staggered so that the screws will not touch each other when they are installed (see **fig. 3**). Drill ¾"-diameter holes, each ¾" deep, followed by ⁷⁄₁₆" pilot holes that extend completely through the post.

3. Cut six horizontal side pieces out of 4 × 4 cedar, each 15½" long. Cut four crosspieces out of 4 × 4 cedar, each 41" long. Sand all the pieces, going from coarse to smooth.

Fig. 2

4×4 POSTS MARKED ON ENDS

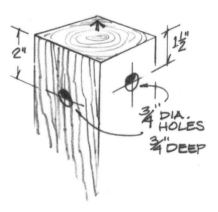

Fig. 3

For a more classical look, rout the top and bottom edges of all the horizontal side pieces, using a quirk and bead router bit.

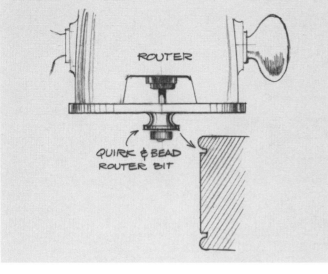

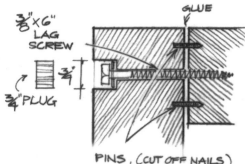

Fig. 5

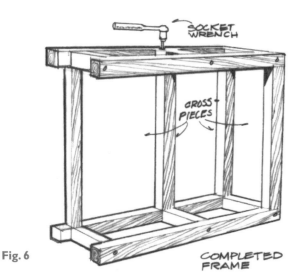

Fig. 6

4. Assemble the sides as shown in **fig. 4**. To do this, stand three horizontal side pieces on end, position a 4 × 4 post on top of them, and glue and screw each joint with a ⅜" × 6" lag screw using a socket wrench. Turn the assembly over and install the second post.

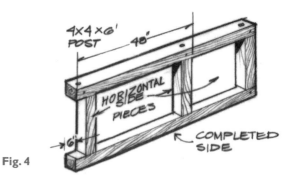

Fig. 4

5. To prevent the 4 × 4 horizontal side pieces from turning once installed, cut the heads off four 2" nails (using a bolt cutter), and hammer them halfway into the side grain of each vertical post. When you screw the post down, these points will press into the soft end grain and will help lock the posts and beams together (see **fig. 5**).

6. Lay one of the assembled sides flat on the ground, and stand the four crosspieces on it, aligning them with the horizontal side pieces. Apply epoxy glue to the exposed ends. With an assistant, carefully position the second side over the ends of the crosspieces (see **fig. 6**). Use three bar clamps to hold the assembly in place, and screw ⅜" × 6" lag screws through the side into the ends of the crosspieces. Turn the assembly over and follow the same procedure for the second side. Stand up the structure. For a finished look, plug the holes and sand them smooth.

Lattice and Siding

1. Measure the uppermost openings in the sides and back of the covered seat. Then, using an electric jig saw, cut the lattice to fit inside the openings. Install the lattice, using ¾" cove molding nailed onto both sides.

2. Install the 1 × 4 V-groove vertical boards in the bottom side and back openings, using ¾" × ¾" cove molding to secure them to the horizontal 4 × 4s.

Roof Frame

1. To make the roof rafters, cut four pieces of 2 × 4, each to a length of 32¼". Cut the ends off each piece at a 30° angle (see **fig. 7**).

2. Measure 1½" up from the bottom end of each piece, and cut a right-angle notch (bird's mouth), 1⅛" × 1⅞" (see detail, **fig. 7**).

3. For the purlins, cut three pieces of 2 × 2 cedar, each 22½" long. Cut a 1½" × 1½" notch in the rafters to accept the 2 × 2 purlins, 1¼" from the bottom ends (see **figs. 7 and 8**). Cut a 1½" notch out of the peak, where the rafters meet, to support the 2 × 2 ridgepole. Glue and screw the pieces together using temporary blocks to keep the rafters from spreading. Make sure the pieces are square with one another and that the inside measurement between the bird's mouth cuts is 48".

4. When the glue has dried, cut two 2 × 2 crossties, each 44" long, and cut the ends off at 30° angles. Glue and screw these two crossties to the bottoms of the rafters. Set the assembled roof frame on the main frame, and secure it by screwing down through the 2 × 2 crossties into the top front and rear 4 × 4s of the frame.

▶ **B U I L D I N G   T I P**

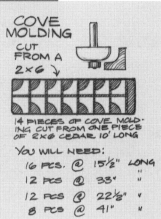

It is much easier to paint the lattice before installing it. If you own a router, it is cheaper and quite easy to make your own cove molding by routing, then ripping, a clear cedar 2 × 6 into ¾" × ¾" strips. You will need about 120' of molding cut to the lengths shown.

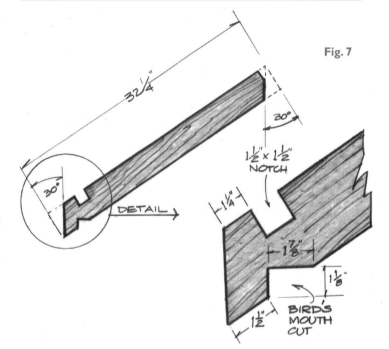

Fig. 7

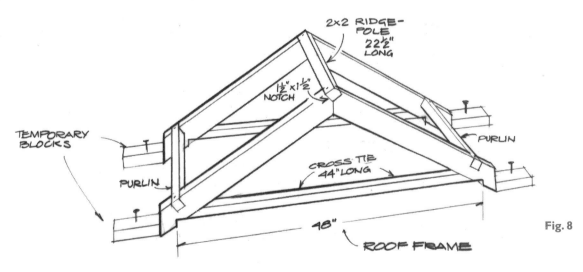

Fig. 8

1x4 RIDGE TRIM

1x2 ROOF SLATS

1x4 FASCIA TRIM ⅛" OVERLAP

LATTICE

Fig. 9

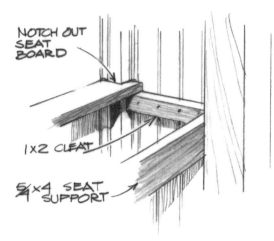

NOTCH OUT SEAT BOARD

1x2 CLEAT

⁵⁄₄ x 4 SEAT SUPPORT

Fig. 10

Roof Trim

1. Referring to **fig. 9,** cut, glue, and nail diagonal cedar lattice to the front and back gables of the roof frame, allowing each piece to overlap the top of the main 4 × 4 frame by 1⅛". Cut off the top of the lattice flush with the tops of the rafters. Trim the front and sides of the roof with clear 1 × 4 cedar, using 2" galvanized finishing nails. Begin with the side trim, nailing it to the ends of the rafters. Next, cut the front trim pieces to meet at the peak, each at a 30° angle; trial fit them together. Hold the front trim pieces in place and mark on the back where the side pieces meet. Cut where marked and nail in place, using 2" galvanized nails spaced 8" apart.

2. Cover the roof with 1 × 2 cedar slats 27½"-long spaced 1" apart and overlapping the front and back fascia trim boards by 1" (see **fig. 6**).

Seat

1. Measure the inside width from side panel to side panel (about 43"), and cut six pieces of ⁵⁄₄ × 4 clear cedar for the seat. Screw one piece to the inside backs of the two front posts, 18" up from the bottom of the posts, so that it provides a lateral support for the seat (see **fig. 6**). Nail one ¾" × 1½" cleat across each side, 18" up from the bottom to support the seat on the sides. Install the remaining ⁵⁄₄ × 4 cedar boards for the seat, using 2" finishing nails nailed to the cleats and the supporting board (see **fig. 10**). The front and back seat boards will have to be notched around the vertical corner posts.

2. For a final elegant touch, chamfer the outside edges of the corner posts with a 45° bevel router bit.

Garden Table

After working in the city all winter, we celebrate the summer months by spending as much time as possible outdoors, working, relaxing, and, of course, dining al fresco. We eat most of our meals at a long table that David built at one end of our garden. When night falls, we illuminate the table with hurricane lanterns, build a wood fire (no charcoal allowed), and cook out as often as possible. Friends and relatives join us on weekends, gathering together at what has become an indispensable landmark representing years of pleasant memories. When the first chill sets in, we bundle up; only when it becomes teeth-chatteringly cold do we reluctantly head indoors to eat.

Qty.	Size	Description	Location or Use
1	10'	6 × 6 redwood	legs
1	6'	2 × 8 redwood	table supports
10	8'	2 × 4 redwood	table top
2 bags	80 lbs.	concrete mix	base collar
1 box	½"	wood plugs	table top
1 box	3"	galvanized deck screws	
1 qt.		water sealer or stain	

When you call your local lumberyard to order the clear redwood 2 × 4s, you may be shocked to hear the price. However, consider what you are getting: a rot-resistant table that (with a little care) will look great and serve you well for many years. Left natural, without paint or stain, the clear redwood weathers to a soft shade of gray and blends in with the surroundings.

Legs

1. Cut the two 59"-long legs out of 6 × 6 lumber. Hold up the butt end of each leg so it is at a slant, and heat with a propane torch. When it begins to smoke, drip candle wax onto the leg bottoms, sealing the wood and creating a moisture barrier that will keep water from wicking up the end grain (see **fig. 1**).

2. The area where the post emerges from the ground is the most vulnerable to rot and insect infestation, so soak this part of each leg with wood preservative. Once it is dry, give it a coat of roofing tar.

3. Using a post-hole digger, dig two holes 32" deep and 54" apart. Place a brick or stone in each hole for the legs to rest on. Do not backfill the holes until both legs have been positioned in the ground and you have checked to make sure that they are square. Place a 2 × 4 across the tops of the posts and check for level, as well. Make sure each leg is 27½" high from the ground, and use the level to check that

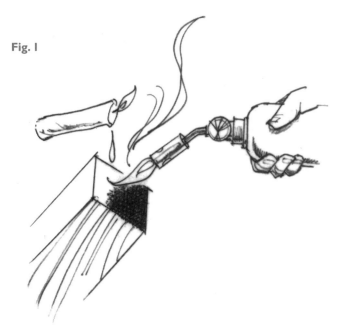

Fig. 1

each leg is plumb. This can be frustrating and time consuming, but it is an important step to ensure that the table remains solid. After each of the legs are positioned perfectly, backfill the holes, tamping down and compressing the loose soil as you fill. Continue checking with a level to make sure the posts do not go out of alignment.

4. Don't fill the hole completely with dirt. The top portion should be filled with concrete. Measure out 4" from each side of each leg, and dig a 3"-deep circular trench around the leg where it meets the ground. Pour a stiff mixture of wet concrete in the top portion of each hole and in the trench around the posts. The diameter of each trench should measure approximately 14". Mound up the concrete with a trowel, creating a collar, so that rainwater will be shed from the surface (see **fig. 2**). Let the concrete set overnight. After several months, the wood may shrink away from the concrete, so apply a bead of caulking where the two materials join.

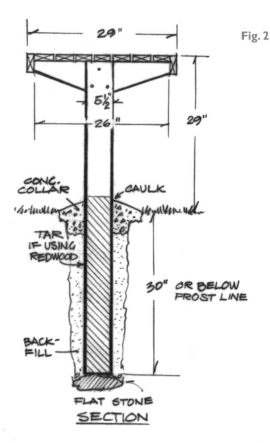

Fig. 2

Table Supports

1. Each table support forms a T across the top of one of the legs and provides a support for the 2 × 4s. Carefully mark a 1½"-wide, 7¼"-deep slot, in the center of the top of each post to accept the table support. Do this by drawing two vertical lines 7¼" down on the outsides of each post. Using a hand saw, make two vertical cuts down each post (see **fig. 3a**). Drill two ½" holes at the bottom of the cuts, and use a ½"-wide chisel to cut out the inside of each slot (see **figs. 3b and 3c**).

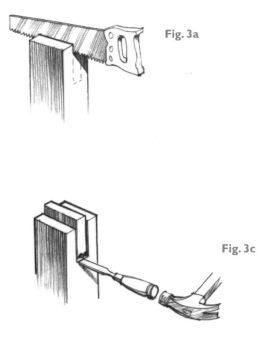

Fig. 3a

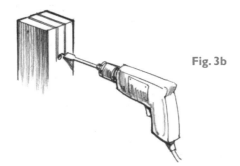

Fig. 3b

Fig. 3c

2. Cut the two table supports out of the 2 × 8, each measuring 26" long. Taper the ends of each support (see **figs. 4a and 4b**). Center the supports in the leg slots, and screw three 3" galvanized deck screws through each side of the legs and into the table supports.

Fig. 4a

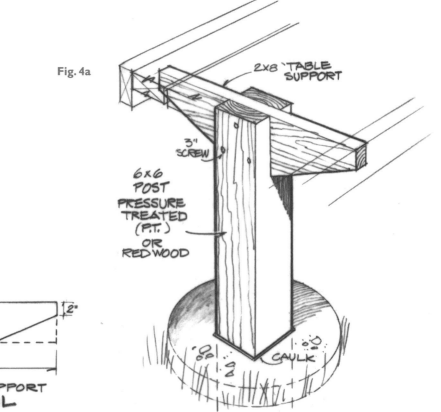

Fig. 4b

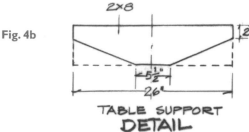

TABLE SUPPORT
DETAIL

Table Top

1. Cut seven redwood 2 × 4s, each 93" long. For the table edging, cut two 29"-long pieces and two 8'-long pieces. Precise measurements are important. Lay the seven 2 × 4s across the two table supports so there is a ¼" space between each one. Draw a centerline across the 2 × 4s above the center of each table support, and drill a ½"-diameter counter-bored hole, ½" deep in the center of each 2 × 4. After checking to make sure the ends are aligned evenly, screw all seven pieces to the table supports (see **fig. 5**).

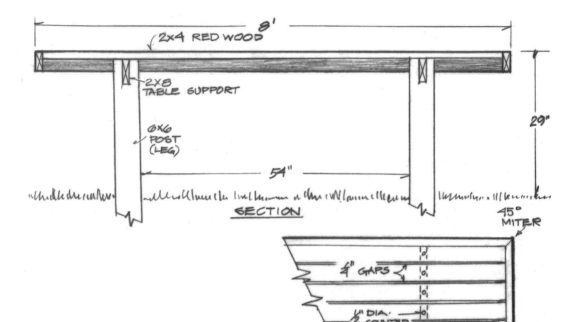

SECTION

PLAN VIEW

Fig. 5

2. Trim off the ends of the table edging at a 45° angle. After drilling ½"-diameter counter-bored holes ¾" down from the top edging, screw the side and end edging to the table top.

Finishing

1. Fill the ½" screw holes with ½" plugs. It is easy and looks better to make your own plugs from a scrap piece of redwood, using a special bit called a plug cutter (see **fig. 6**) that can only be used with a drill press. If you don't have access to a drill press and a plug cutter, you can buy birch or cherry wood plugs to fit the holes. If these aren't available locally, you can order them from any good woodworking supply catalog. Glue and gently tap the plugs in place with a wooden mallet. Using medium (80-grit) sandpaper, smooth the tops of the plugs flush with the table surface.

2. Allow redwood to weather for a week or two, and then give it a coat of sealer, such as CWF or Thompson's Weatherseal. Each year the table top will become a little grayer. If you don't like a weathered look, it can easily be lightly sanded and covered with a coat of sealer to keep the rich-looking redwood finish.

Fig. 6

Garden Bench

A garden bench has many uses. It can be situated at the end of a garden path, provide a place to rest after a few hours of weeding and planting, or serve as a sturdy seat to accompany a picnic table. The following design is for a simple, durable, well-constructed bench that takes only a few hours to construct. The seat is 48" long, and the legs are freestanding. Depending upon your needs, you can change the dimensions of the bench.

Qty.	Size	Description	Location or Use
1	8'	4 × 8 fir or P.T. timber	seat
1	10'	2 × 6 P.T. lumber	legs and crosspieces
2	15"	⅜" diameter threaded rod, with 4 washers and 4 nuts	
1 lb.	2½"	galvanized deck screws	

Seat

1. Cut two pieces of 4 × 8, each 48" long. (You might have to use a handsaw if your electric circular saw does not reach all the way through the 4 × 8.) Make two marks on each 4 × 8, one 6" in from the end and the other 10½" in from the end (see **fig. 1a**). Mark the same dimensions on the opposite end of each 4 × 8. Cut two notches, 1½" deep by 4½" wide, out of the inside face of each 4 × 8, where you have marked. This distance is the same width as the bench legs. Make the notches by resting the timber on edge and cutting several 1½" deep cuts inside the marked area. Draw a straight line from the bottom of one cut to the bottom of the other cut.

2. Lay the timber down flat and chisel out the notch, using a sharp ¾" wide chisel (see **fig. 1b**). Chiseling out the notched material is best done by holding the chisel against the pencil line, with the bevel side of the chisel facing the wood that you will be removing. Give two or three hard blows to the wood, incising a line approximately ¼" deep. Turn the timber over and do the same on the other side. Turn the timber on edge and chip away the inside material (see **fig. 1c**).

Legs

1. Cut six pieces of 2 × 6 P.T. lumber, 16" long (four for the legs, and two for the crosspieces). Cut two pieces of P.T. lumber, both 10½" long, for the inside pieces of the legs.

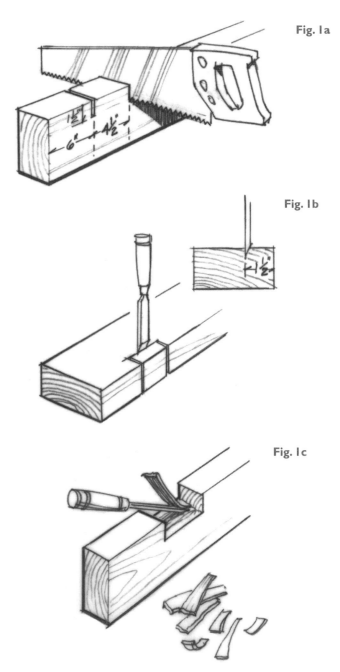

Fig. 1a

Fig. 1b

Fig. 1c

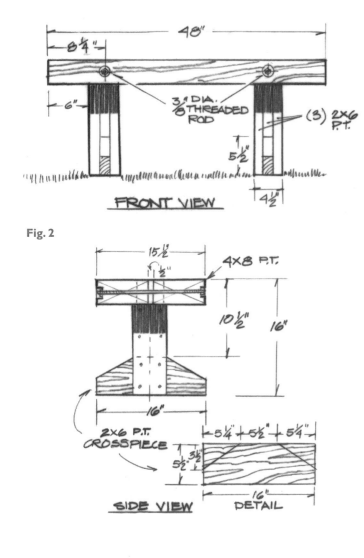

FRONT VIEW

Fig. 2

SIDE VIEW

DETAIL

2. To cut the leg cross-pieces, make diagonal cuts on two corners of each of the two 16"-long 2 × 6s (see detail, **fig. 2,** for the exact dimensions).

3. To construct each leg, sandwich a 10½"-long 2 × 6 and a base crosspiece between two 16"-long 2 × 6s. Fasten the pieces together using eight 2½" galvanized deck screws, placed in each leg support (see side view, **fig. 2,** for the exact dimensions).

4. Cut out two shoulder notches in each leg support to accommodate the bench seat. Using a carpenter's square, mark a 1" × 3½" shoulder notch on each side of each leg. Make a 1"-deep crosscut 3½" down from the top, and chisel out the notch (see **fig. 3**).

5. The leg supports are attached to each end of the bench top by a 15½"-long, ⅜"-diameter threaded rod. Use a 1½"-diameter spade bit to bore a 1"-deep hole 8¼" in from each end of the bench. With the bench laid on its side, trial fit the two timbers to the legs, and mark where the hole for the rod should go by tapping the threaded rod a few times to make a dent in the leg. Use this mark as a guide to drill a ½"-diameter hole through each seat timber and through the top of the leg. Note that the larger (½") hole is necessary to adjust for any mis-alignment. Assemble the pieces and slip the threaded rod through them, tightening the nuts with a socket wrench.

Fig. 3

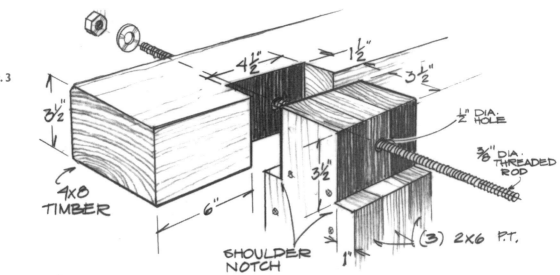

Garden Heart Stool

Every now and then it's nice to sit down, relax, and survey what you have accomplished in the garden while planning for the next season. It is also helpful to have a place to rest your tools where they won't be over-looked and mistakenly left outside overnight. This garden stool serves both purposes. It also makes a handy stepping stool when pruning hard-to-reach branches and can even serve as an extra seat for unexpected guests at the end of your picnic table. Sturdy yet lightweight, the stool can easily be moved about, using the heart shaped cut-out as a comfort-able hand grip.

Qty.	Size	Description	Location or Use
1	2'	1 × 12 clear cedar	seat
1	2'	2 × 4 cedar	support cleats
1	6'	2 × 2 cedar	legs
12	2"	galvanized deck screws	
1 qt.		water sealer	

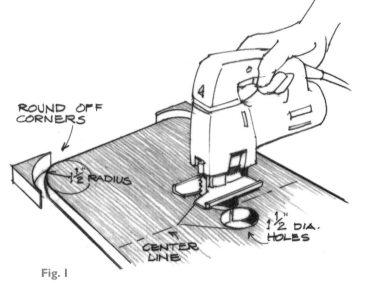

ROUND OFF CORNERS

1½" RADIUS

CENTER LINE

1½" DIA. HOLES

Fig. 1

Fig. 2

2"

2"

Seat

Make the seat by cutting the 1 × 12 piece of cedar to a length of 22". To cut the heart-shaped hole in the seat, find the center of the board and drill two 1½"-diameter holes, each centered ¾" from either side of the center of the board (see **fig. 1**). Draw two tangent intersecting lines from the outside of the two circles, meeting below the circles. Cut out the remaining triangular piece of wood using a jig saw. Cut the seat corners at a 1½" radius, rounding off the edges with sandpaper (see **fig. 1**).

Support Cleats

1. To make the two leg support cleats, cut two 10"-long pieces of cedar 2 × 4s. Using a table saw or block plane, bevel the edges at an 11° angle. Mark where the center of the 1½"-diameter leg holes will be by measuring in 2" from each corner to the centerline of each support cleat (see **fig. 2**).

2. The legs are attached to the 2 × 4 support cleats so that they slant out at an 11° angle on either side. Use a 1½" spade drill bit to make the four angled leg holes in the 2 × 4 support cleats (see **fig. 3a**). Use this book as a visual guide to help eyeball the angle of the drill while cutting (see **fig. 3b**). Start the hole with the drill held vertically, and then gradually slant the drill to an 11° angle while drilling all the way through.

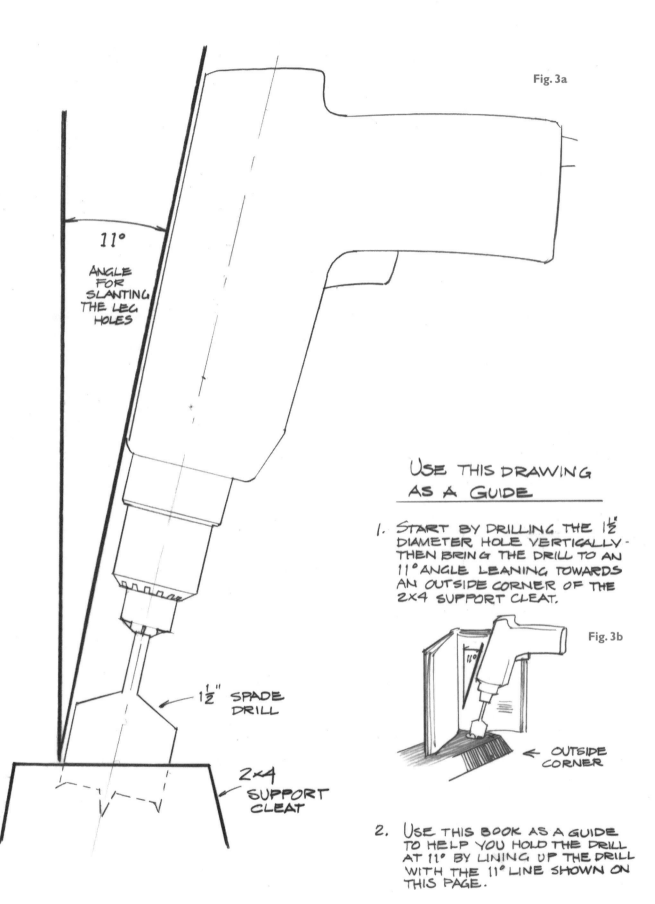

11°

ANGLE
FOR
SLANTING
THE LEG
HOLES

1½" SPADE
DRILL

2×4
SUPPORT
CLEAT

USE THIS DRAWING
AS A GUIDE

1. START BY DRILLING THE 1½"
DIAMETER HOLE VERTICALLY -
THEN BRING THE DRILL TO AN
11° ANGLE LEANING TOWARDS
AN OUTSIDE CORNER OF THE
2×4 SUPPORT CLEAT.

Fig. 3b

11°

OUTSIDE
CORNER

2. USE THIS BOOK AS A GUIDE
TO HELP YOU HOLD THE DRILL
AT 11° BY LINING UP THE DRILL
WITH THE 11° LINE SHOWN ON
THIS PAGE.

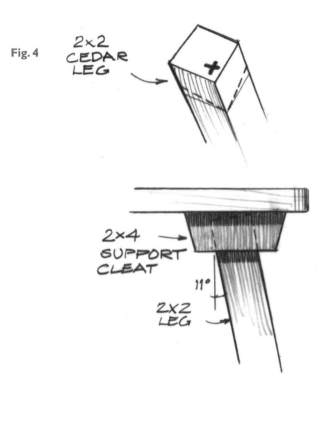

Fig. 4

2×2
CEDAR
LEG

2×4
SUPPORT
CLEAT

11°

2×2
LEG

Legs

1. Make the legs by cutting four pieces of 2 × 2 cedar, each 15 " long. Draw a line around the perimeter of each leg, 1½ " from one end. The object of this step is to round the ends of the square 2 × 2 legs, with a shoulder that conforms to the 11° angle of the leg.

2. Place an X on what will be the top outside corner of each 2 × 2 to indicate which way the leg will eventually face once the seat is completed (see **fig. 4**). To make the legs fit into the angled holes, the corners of the 2 × 2 must also be cut off at an 11° angle. Draw a line, slanted 11° from the existing line, and use a hand saw to crosscut the corners around the legs. Use a vice to hold each leg, and use a chisel and hammer to split off the corners of each one (see **fig. 5**). Round off the ends with a rasp until

SPLITTING OFF
CORNERS

Fig. 5

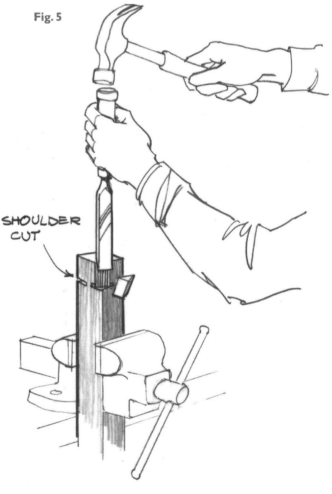

SHOULDER
CUT

they fit in the 1½"-diameter holes (see **fig. 6**). You should be able to twist them by hand into the holes, so that they fit snugly. Do not pound them with a hammer because you might split the 2 × 4 leg support. When you are satisfied that they fit together perfectly, glue the legs into the holes.

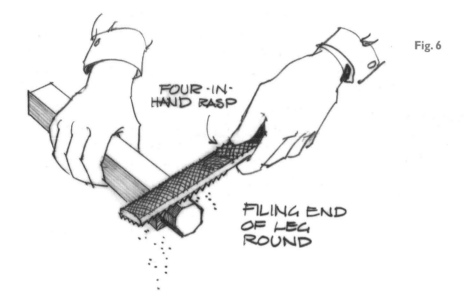

FOUR-IN-HAND RASP

FILING END OF LEG ROUND

Fig. 6

3. Join the four 2 × 4 leg supports to the underside of the seat, ¾" in from the outside edges of the seat, using six 2" galvanized deck screws (see **fig. 7**). Give the stool a coat of water sealer to protect it and to bring out the rich, natural color of the cedar.

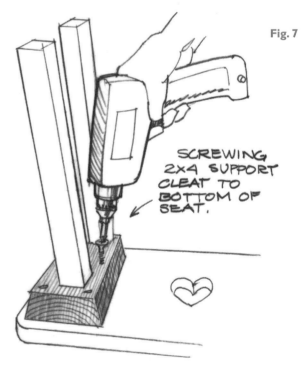

Fig. 7

SCREWING 2x4 SUPPORT CLEAT TO BOTTOM OF SEAT.

Viewing Pergola

This viewing pergola was designed and built for some friends with property overlooking Three Mile Harbor on the end of Long Island. They needed a comfortable, protected seat to relax in and enjoy their spectacular waterfront view, and this was the perfect solution. They have trained wisteria to cover the latticed sides, and in the spring it is enveloped with fragrant purple blossoms. The pergola is simple to construct, and it is designed to withstand high winds. Although we built this one out of clear cedar and lauan, you can use a less expensive type of lumber and cut the cost in half. The lattice can be purchased at your lumber store and comes in convenient 4' × 8' sheets. We recommend using heavy duty ⅜" lattice rather than the cheaper lightweight variety, which is too flimsy for this project.

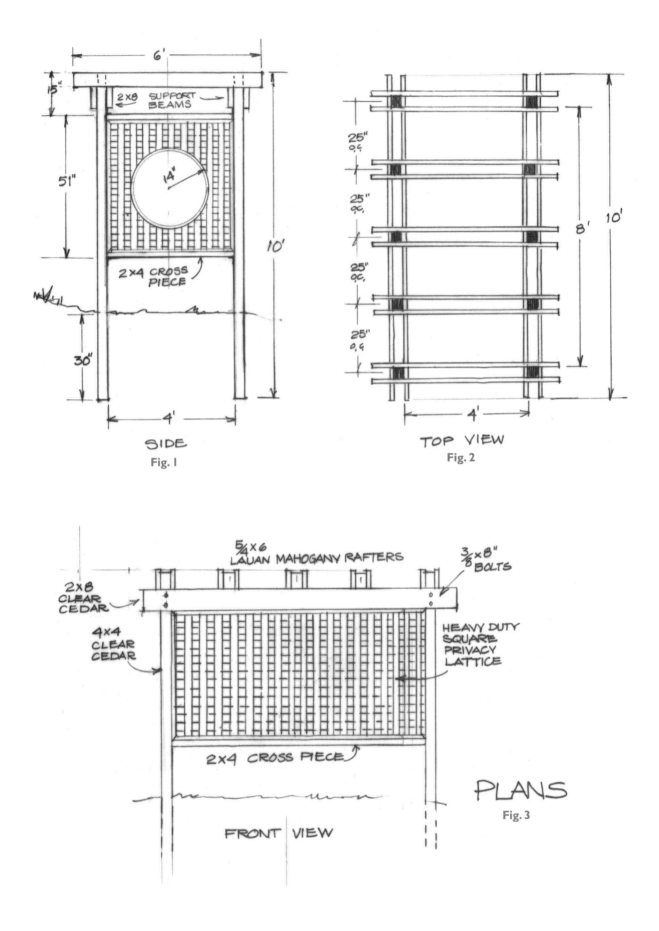

6'

15"

2×8 SUPPORT BEAMS

51"

14"

2×4 CROSS PIECE

30"

4'

10'

SIDE

Fig. I

25" O.C.

25" O.C.

25" O.C.

25" O.C.

25" O.C.

8'

10'

4'

TOP VIEW

Fig. 2

5/4 × 6 LAUAN MAHOGANY RAFTERS

3/8 × 8" BOLTS

2×8 CLEAR CEDAR

4×4 CLEAR CEDAR

HEAVY DUTY SQUARE PRIVACY LATTICE

2×4 CROSS PIECE

PLANS

Fig. 3

FRONT VIEW

Materials Needed

Qty.	Size	Description	Location or Use
4	10'	4 × 4 clear cedar	corner posts
4	10'	2 × 8 clear cedar	support beams
10	6'	⁵⁄₄ × 6 lauan	rafters
4	4'	2 × 4 clear cedar	side cross-pieces
2	8'	2 × 4 clear cedar	rear cross-pieces
2	4' × 8'	heavy-duty square lattice	sides and rear
I	6'	4 × 4 #2 cedar	interlocking blocks
14	¾" × ¾" × 8'	clear cedar	lattice cleat strips
12	6'	1 × 2 #2 spruce	temporary post supports
2	12'	³⁄₁₆" × 1" cedar lattice strips	frames for circle cut-out
8	⅜" × 8"	galvanized bolts, nuts, washers	corner posts
I lb.	3½"	galvanized deck screws	interlocking blocks
I box	1¼"	galvanized finishing nails	lattice cleats
12	3"	Tetco Kant Sag C3	post connector angle brackets
I box	¾"	brass brads	circular window frame
I qt.		stain or water seal	

Begin by clearing the site and laying out the location for the posts (refer to Setting Corner Markers on page 10). The measurements are for the 4'-long distance *between* the posts, not to the *center* of the posts. Because lattice comes in 4'-divisible increments, this allows the lattice to fit perfectly between the posts, minimizing cutting.

Installing the Posts

Dig four 30"-deep holes for the posts (refer to Posts and Gates on page 7). Place the posts in the holes and level the post tops, using a line level and string. Once the posts are plumb, hold them in position temporarily, using three 1 × 2s at each post (see **fig. 4**). Don't backfill the soil around the posts until the pergola is completed.

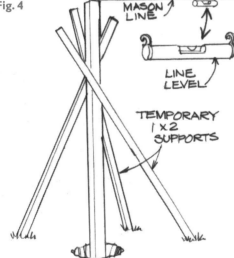

Fig. 4

MASON LINE

LINE LEVEL

TEMPORARY 1 × 2 SUPPORTS

Attaching Crosspieces

Cut four 2 × 4s, each 48⅛" long, allowing clearance for the lattice to fit inside the 4 × 4s. (Lumber is generally, but not always, sold a little longer than specified to allow for damage to the ends.) Attach the crosspieces to the support posts, using 3"-long angle brackets. Screw the angle brackets first to the 2 × 4s, setting each bracket back ¹⁄₁₆" from the end of the 2 × 4, so that when the other half of the bracket is screwed to the post, it will be drawn up snugly against the post. Reinforce the 2 × 4s by counter-sinking two 3½" galvanized screws at an angle into the posts (see **fig. 5**).

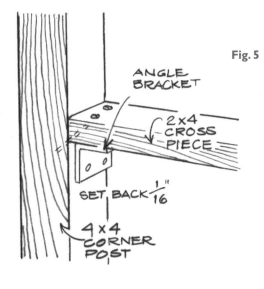

Fig. 5

ANGLE BRACKET

2×4 CROSS PIECE

SET BACK ¹⁄₁₆"

4×4 CORNER POST

Installing the Lattice

Make a frame for the lattice by cutting the ¾" × ¾" cedar cleat strips to length. Bevel the ends at a 45° angle, so that they will fit together neatly in the corners. Frame the inside of the sides and back, nailing the cedar strips to the 2 × 4s and posts with 1¼" galvanized nails (see **fig. 6**). Cut one piece of lattice in half to make the two sides of the pergola, and use 1¼" nails to secure the lattice to the frame. Install the back of the pergola, using a full 4' × 8' sheet of lattice. Frame the outside of the lattice to hold it firmly between the two cedar frames.

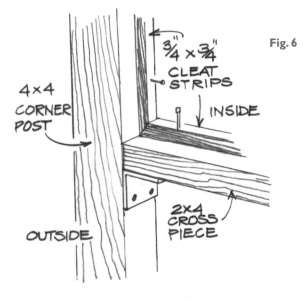

Fig. 6

¾" × ¾" CLEAT STRIPS

INSIDE

4×4 CORNER POST

OUTSIDE

2×4 CROSS PIECE

Attaching the Support Beams

Measure down 15" from the top of each post, and place a mark where the bottom of each 2 × 8 support beam will go. Clamp each pair of beams to the posts, and bore ⅜"-diameter holes through the beams, into the center of the posts, and into the other beam (see **fig. 7**). Bolt the beams to the post, using ⅜" washers and nuts.

Fig. 7

2×8 SUPPORT BEAMS

⅜" AUGER BIT

Interlocking Blocks

Cut six 4 × 4 blocks, each 12" long. Place three blocks between each pair of support beams, 25" on center. Place the ten rafters on top of

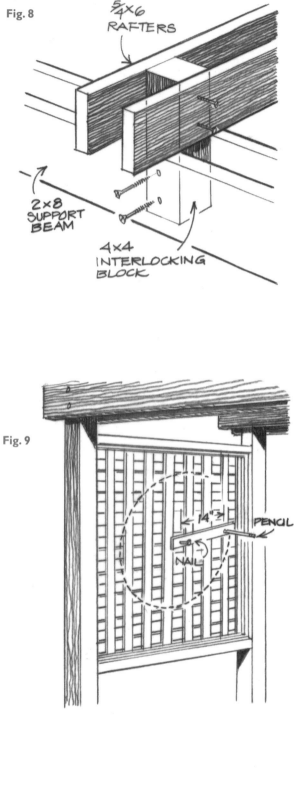

Fig. 8

5/4 × 6 RAFTERS

2 × 8 SUPPORT BEAM

4 × 4 INTERLOCKING BLOCK

Fig. 9

14"

PENCIL

NAIL

the support beams, straddling the 4 × 4 blocks; screw them together using 3½" deck screws. These interlocking blocks hold the rafters and the support beams together, strengthening and stabilizing the entire structure (see **fig. 8**).

Circular Openings

1. To make the circular window openings, you'll need to cut out a circle on each side piece of lattice. Make a measuring stick out of a scrap piece of lumber and, with a nail in one end (placed at the center of the piece of lattice) and a pencil hole 14" from the nail, draw a 28"-diameter circle (see **fig. 9**). Cut the circle out, using an electric jig saw.

2. Soften the ³⁄₁₆" × 1" cedar strips by soaking them in hot water overnight. Bend them into the circular holes in the lattice, and secure them with ¾" brass brads (see **fig. 10**).

3. Place a bench inside the pergola, and train a climbing vine over the lattice.

CUT WHERE STRIPS OVERLAP

Fig. 10

Deck with Bench & Umbrella

Find a spot in your backyard or garden that is secluded from the house and the rest of the garden, and build this small deck as a retreat; a place to read, relax, and meditate. Surround the deck on three sides with rambling rugosa roses, which will offer their benefits year-round — scent and blooms throughout the summer, rose-hips in the fall, and little if no maintenance. Or, build the deck on low, poorly drained soil in an area that you would otherwise not be able to use, and surround it with iris, grasses, cat tails, and other aquatic plants. A deck for these purposes need not be big — in fact, an 8' × 8' square is a practical size. Both rot-resistant cedar and redwood are good choices for materials, and both will weather to a soft gray, blending with the surrounding woods and plantings. The deck includes a U-shaped bench, just the right size to accommodate a 5'-diameter table and an 8' umbrella. The two rear corners of the bench allow ample space for large pots to be planted with shrubs or flowers.

Fig. I

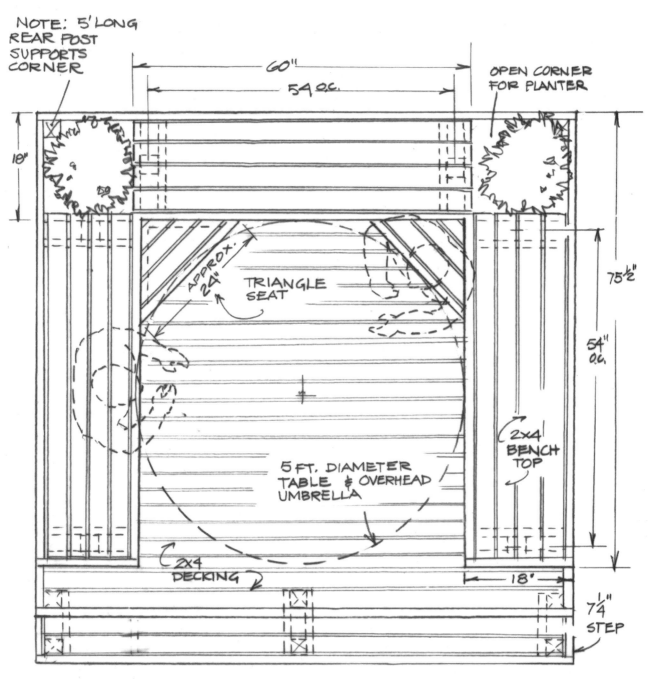

NOTE: 5' LONG
REAR POST
SUPPORTS
CORNER

60"

54 O.C.

OPEN CORNER
FOR PLANTER

18"

TRIANGLE
SEAT

APPROX. 24"

75½"

54" O.C.

2X4
BENCH
TOP

5 FT. DIAMETER
TABLE & OVERHEAD
UMBRELLA

2X4
DECKING

18"

7¼"
STEP

PLAN VIEW
DECK & BENCH

Qty.	Size	Description	Location or Use
4	8'	2 × 8 #2 cedar	deck frame
2	4'	4 × 4 #2 cedar	deck frame posts
8	5'	4 × 4 #2 cedar	seating posts
3	1'	4 × 4 #2 cedar	step posts
4	8'	2 × 6 #2 const. fir	deck joists
2	8'	2 × 4 #2 const. fir	deck ledges
1	4'	2 × 4 #2 const. fir	step support blocks
1	12'	2 × 6 #2 const. fir	front step
26	8'	2 × 4 #2 cedar	decking and steps
5	8'	2 × 4 #2 cedar	seat frames
1	5'	2 × 4 #2 cedar	seat front
12	5'	2 × 4 #2 cedar	seat decking
2	18"	2 × 4 #2 cedar	seat ends
2	10'	2 × 4 #2 cedar	triangle seats
6	5'	2 × 4 #2 cedar	seat supports and deck cleats
2 lbs.	3"	galvanized deck screws	deck

Deck

Since the deck will be built on posts, it is not necessary to make the building site perfectly level. Begin by screwing two 96"-long 2 × 8s to two 93"-long 2 × 8s in order to form a perfect 8'-square frame. The front and rear pieces overlap the side pieces. Make sure the deck frame is absolutely square by measuring the diagonals, which should be 135¾" from outside corner to outside corner. Mark the soil directly below each inside corner, and dig four 30"-deep holes. Cut the 4 × 4 posts so that they are 1½" below the top edge of the deck frame, and place them in the holes. Screw the deck frame to the posts, using 3" galvanized deck screws. Dig two more holes and install two additional posts for the front and rear deck frame pieces (see **fig. 2**).

Locating the Seating Posts

Measure in 10¼" from the front and rear corners and make a mark. Measure in 10¾" from the first

Fig. 2

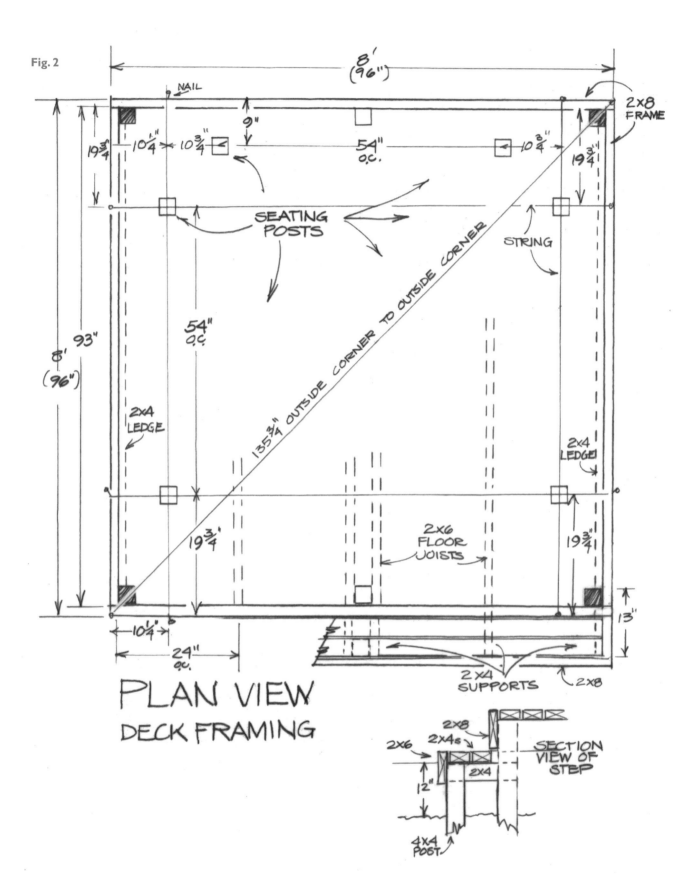

PLAN VIEW
DECK FRAMING

mark and make another mark. Tie strings to temporary nails placed at these points, and draw the strings across the deck frame, attaching them at the other side. Measure 19¾" from the rear and front corners along the side deck frame pieces; mark the spots and attach strings. Dig post holes directly below where the strings intersect, and install the posts into the holes, allowing 15½" of the posts to extend above the strings. After checking to make sure that all the seating posts are at the same height and are at right angles with each other, backfill the post holes (see **fig. 2**).

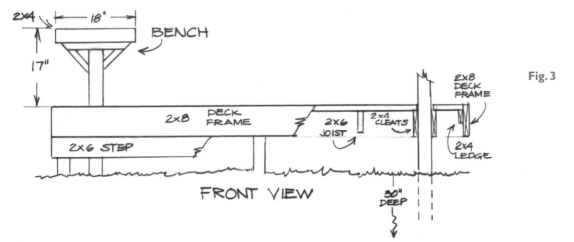

Fig. 3

Floor Joists

Join four 2 × 6 floor joists to the 2 × 8 front and rear deck frame, allowing a 1½" space on top for the 2 × 4 decking. Attach an 86"-long 2 × 4 ledge to each side of the frame to support the ends of the 2 × 4 decking (see **figs. 2 and 3**).

Decking

Install the 2 × 4 decking, using 16d galvanized nails or 3" galvanized deck screws. Screw short, 2 × 4 cleats to the seating posts to support the decking where it meets the posts. Allow ¼" spacing between each 2 × 4 (see **fig. 4**).

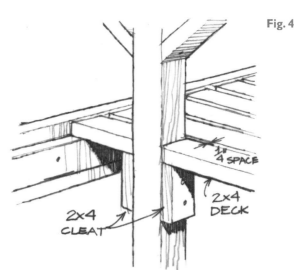

Fig. 4

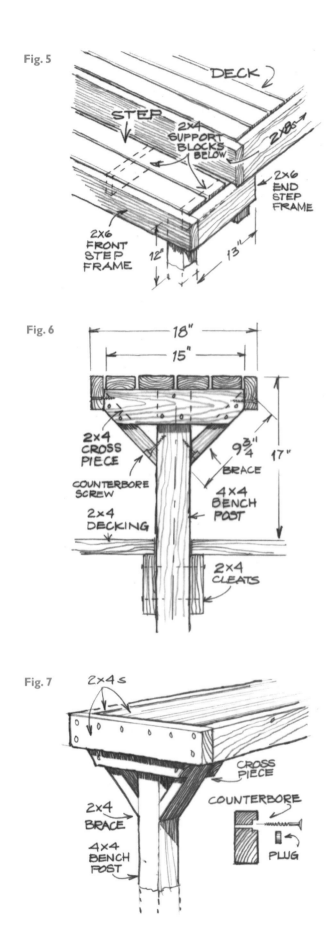

Fig. 5

DECK

STEP

2×4 SUPPORT BLOCKS BELOW

2×8s

2×6 END STEP FRAME

2×6 FRONT STEP FRAME

12"

13"

Fig. 6

18"

15"

2×4 CROSS PIECE

COUNTERBORE SCREW

2×4 DECKING

9¾"

17"

BRACE

4×4 BENCH POST

2×4 CLEATS

Fig. 7

2×4s

CROSS PIECE

COUNTERBORE

2×4 BRACE

4×4 BENCH POST

PLUG

Step

Frame the step by screwing two 13"-long 2 × 6 pieces to each side corner post. Attach a 4 × 4 post, 12" long, to the loose end of each step frame. Nail an 8'-long 2 × 6 across the front of the step. Add another 4 × 4 post in the middle and six 2 × 4 support blocks equidistant apart. Nail the two deck boards to the support blocks (see **fig. 5**).

Benches

1. The benches are built out of clear cedar or redwood, supported by ∨-wingshaped braces and crosspieces (see **fig. 6**). Cut 12 pieces of 2 × 4, each to a length of 15", for the crosspieces, and 12 pieces, 9¾" long, for the braces. Bevel the ends of the braces at a 45° angle. Screw the crosspieces to the outside of each bench post. Fit the braces between the crosspieces, and use 3½" galvanized deck screws to join them together. Counterbore and screw the bottom of the braces to the bench post (see **fig. 6**).

2. Drill ½"-diameter counterbore holes in the 72½"-long 2 × 4 bench framing boards, and screw them to the front and back of the seats. Add 18"-long 2 × 4 end boards, and plug the counterbore screw holes with ½" plugs cut from a scrap board of the same lumber used for the seating. Attach the remaining four 2 × 4 seating boards, leaving a ¼" space between each board (see **fig. 7**).

3. Build the triangular seats by attaching 15"-long 2 × 4 ledge pieces to the inside corners of the three benches. Screw 2 × 4s, with the ends cut at 45° angles, to the support ledges. Provide a front edge frame for the triangular seats, using a 2 × 4 mitered 45° at both ends (see **fig. 2**). These triangular seats add rigidity to the side seats and also help define the spaces for potted plants.

Garden Swing

Sitting in a garden swing that hangs from a strong tree at the edge of a garden is a relaxing way of viewing your garden while planning for next year's plantings. A garden swing can be made out of stock 2 × 4s and one 2 × 8 found at your local lumberyard or home center. Although cypress would be the wood of choice, for economical reasons the swing can also be built out of common fir construction lumber and then stained or painted for color. If you are using cypress, we suggest allowing it to weather to a soft gray and become an inconspicuous part of the environment. No special skills or tools are required to construct this swing. If you are feeling romantic, use a jig saw to cut out a heart from the back support and hope your partner gets the idea.

Qty.	Size	Description	Location or Use
3	8'	2 x 4 clear redwood	crosspieces, front and rear frame, posts, and arms
3	8'	⅝" x 4' clear redwood	seat
1	5'	2 x 8 clear redwood	backboard
5	30"	¾"-diameter wood dowel	
1 box	2"	galvanized deck screws	
1 box	3"	galvanized deck screws	
2	3"	½" eye bolts	rear posts
2	2"	½" eye bolts	front posts
2	*	½" eye bolts	tree limb
4	½"	galvanized thimbles	
1	approx. 50'**	½"-diameter nylon rope	

*depends on thickness of branch

**height of branch determines length of rope

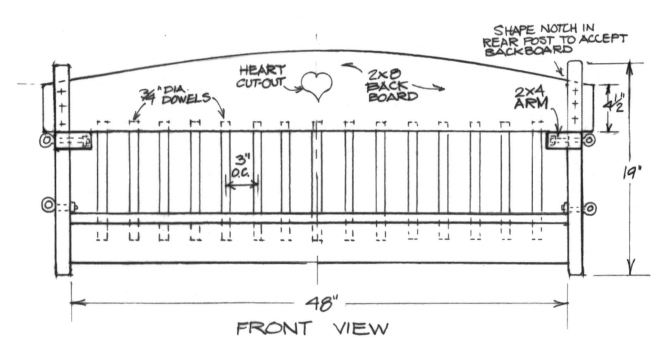

FRONT VIEW

Fig. 1

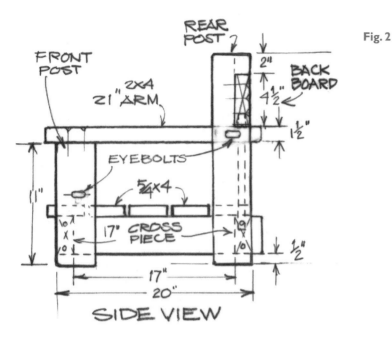

Fig. 2

FRONT POST

REAR POST

2×4 21" ARM

BACK BOARD

2"

4½"

1½"

EYEBOLTS

5/4×4

17" CROSS PIECE

11"

6 X 10

6 X 10

½"

17"

20"

SIDE VIEW

Frame

1. Begin building the seat frame by cutting and screwing two 48"-long 2 × 4s to three 17"-long 2 × 4 crosspieces (see **fig. 3**).

2. Cut and screw five ⁵⁄₄" × 4' seat boards, each 48" long, to the frame. Cut and screw two 11"-long 2 × 4 front posts to the sides, allowing ½" to extend below the crosspieces.

3. To make the rear posts, cut out a 4½" × 1½"-wide notch in each of two 19"-long 2 × 4s, 2" from the top. Screw these rear posts to the side crosspieces (see **fig. 4**).

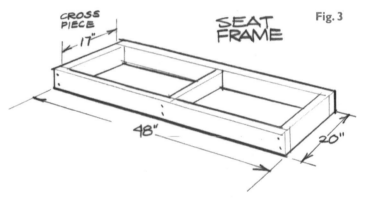

CROSS PIECE

17"

SEAT FRAME

Fig. 3

48"

20"

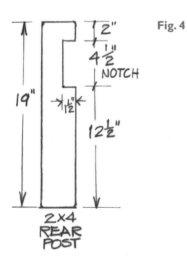

Fig. 4

2"

4½" NOTCH

19"

1½"

12½"

2×4 REAR POST

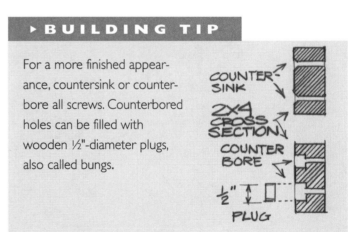

▶ BUILDING TIP

For a more finished appearance, countersink or counterbore all screws. Counterbored holes can be filled with wooden ½"-diameter plugs, also called bungs.

COUNTERSINK

2×4 CROSS SECTION

COUNTERBORE

½"

PLUG

Backboard

1. Use a thin 72"-long stick as a guide to draw the top curve of the backboard. Measure up 4½" from each end of the backboard and temporarily attach a nail. Place a third nail in the center top of the board. Bend the flexible stick around the nails, and draw the shape of a soft curve. Use an electric jig saw to cut the curve, and smooth off the edges with a plane and sandpaper (see **fig. 5**). If desired, cut out a heart as shown in the heart detail (see **fig. 6**).

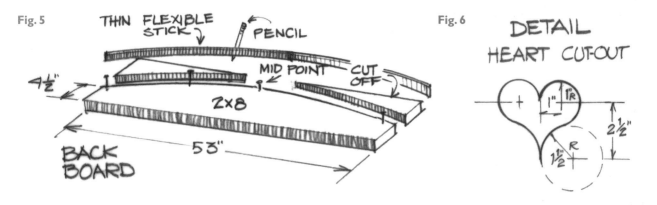

Fig. 5

THIN FLEXIBLE STICK

PENCIL

MID POINT

CUT OFF

2×8

4½"

BACK BOARD

53"

Fig. 6

DETAIL HEART CUT-OUT

1" 1"R

2½"

1½"R

2. Line up the midpoint of the backboard with the midpoint of the seat frame, and make a mark every 3" for the back dowels. Drill a ¾" hole, 1" deep, at each mark. Drill corresponding holes 2" deep through the seat into the frame. Place the 10"-long, ¾"-diameter dowels in the holes, and fit the backboard over the tops of the dowels and into the two rear post notches. Screw the backboard to the rear posts (see **fig. 7**).

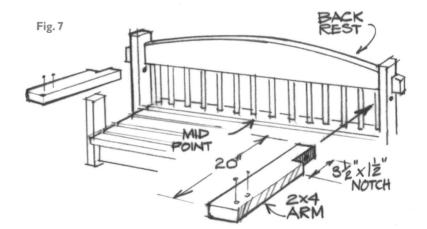

Fig. 7

BACK REST

MID POINT

20"

3½"×1½" NOTCH

2×4 ARM

Arms

Cut two 20"-long arms from a 2 x 4, and make a 3½" x 1½" notch at one end of each arm to fit the rear posts. Screw the arms onto the front and rear posts. Round off the arms with a jig saw or rasp, and sand the wood until it is smooth (see **fig. 8**).

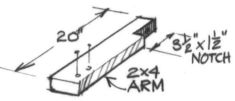

Fig. 8

Eye Bolts

Attach one eye bolt to each of the front and back posts (see **fig. 2**). Recess the nuts and washers of the rear eye bolts by counterboring.

Installation

Hang the swing from a tree that has a strong low branch reaching out 8' to 10'. Drill two holes slightly larger than a ½" eye bolt vertically through the branch, 48" apart. Insert a thimble into each eye bolt to keep the rope from rubbing (see **figs. 9 and 10**). Thread a rope through each eye bolt in the branch, and knot the rope under the thimble. Attach the loose ends of the rope to the eye bolt, securing each with a stop knot.

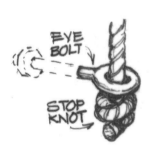

Fig. 9

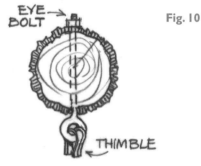

Fig. 10

Special Places in the Garden

Special — Distinguished or different from what is ordinary or usual.
Extraordinary, exceptional.

—Random House Dictionary

Rose Arbor

An arbor not only functions as an overhead support for climbing flowers or vines, but also creates a spot of shade in an otherwise sunny garden. When designing and positioning an arbor, consider both the layout of your garden and also the architecture of your house. An arbor can cover a walkway or path, or it can connect a row of low shrubs or fencing. The arbor that we built was designed to be the focus of the garden. It stands alone with no climbers planted below it, creating a frame for a palette of colors in a background garden.

Fig. I

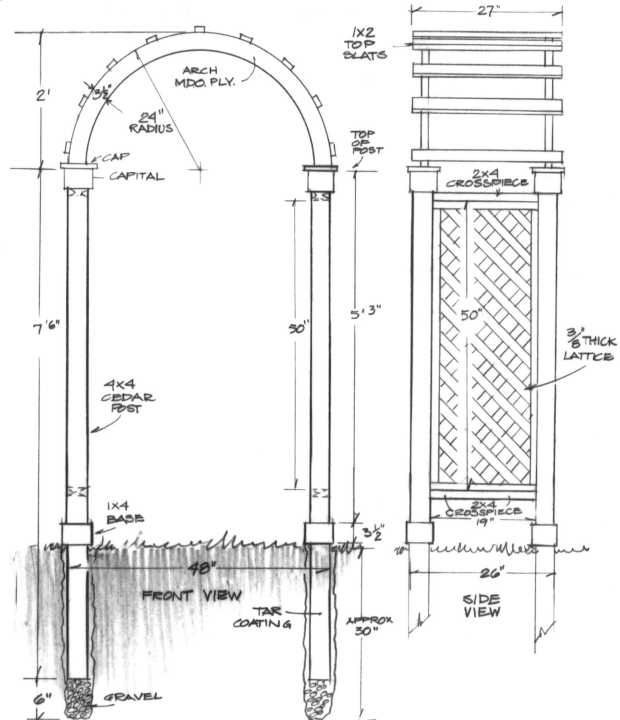

2'

3½"

ARCH
MDO. PLY.

24"
RADIUS

CAP
CAPITAL

TOP
OF
POST

5'3"

50"

7'6"

4X4
CEDAR
POST

1X4
BASE

48"

3½"

FRONT VIEW

TAR
COATING

APPROX
30"

6"   GRAVEL

1X2
TOP
SLATS

27"

2X4
CROSSPIECE

50"

3/8" THICK
LATTICE

2X4
CROSSPIECE
19"

26"

SIDE
VIEW

Qty.	Size	Description	Location or Use
4	8'	4 × 4 clear cedar	posts
I	4' × 8' sheet	M.D.O. plywood	arches
2	8'	I × 4 clear cedar	bases and capitals
I	8'	2 × 4 clear cedar	arch veneer and top slats
I	8'	2 × 4 clear cedar	crosspieces
I	4' × 4' panel	clear cedar privacy lattice	sides
3	8'	2 × 2 clear cedar lattice cap	sides
I6	3½"	galvanized deck screws	
I lb.	2"	galvanized deck screws	
I lb.	I½"	galvanized finishing nails	
I qt.		epoxy glue or 8 oz. waterproof yellow glue	
I	50 ft.	heavy hemp twine	
3	sheets	coarse, medium, and fine sandpaper	

Posts

Begin by cutting four 4 × 4 cedar posts to exactly 7' lengths. Sand the posts using two grades of sandpaper, and fill any holes with wood filler. Using a sharp hand saw, mark and cut out a notch 4" deep by 1½" wide from one end of each post. This is where the ends of the arches will be inserted.

Arches

The arches are generally the most difficult section of any arbor to construct. Traditionally, they are made by cutting, clamping, and gluing many little pieces of wood together and then shaping them into a semicircle. The method we use is much easier, less time consuming, has no joints, and is much stronger. The trick is to use a relatively new plywood called M.D.O. (medium density overlay), or Duraply. This is a product originally developed for highway signs. It has a brown covering, which is actually

To make more accurate cuts, try to line up visually the top and end of the cuts as you are making them (see **fig. 2a**).

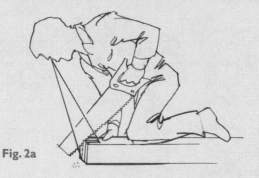

Fig. 2a

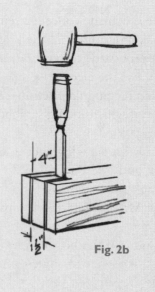

Fig. 2b

Don't worry if the notches aren't perfect, since they will be hidden by the capitals at the top of the posts. To remove the material between the two cuts, use a sharp chisel and a mallet. This is easily done by holding the chisel vertically over the bottom line of the notch and striking it with a mallet (see **fig. 2b**).

Remove the chisel and place it in the end of the post, and give the chisel a series of sharp blows. This will split out about ¼" of wood each time (see **fig. 2c**).

Fig. 2c

Fig. 3

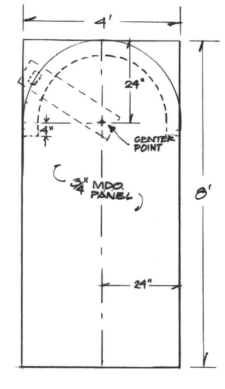

several thin layers of paper impregnated with a phenolic plastic, which makes it impervious to the weather.

1. Each arch consists of two pieces of ¾" M.D.O. plywood that are glued together. Lay the M.D.O. plywood panel on two saw horses and mark a line lengthwise down the center of the panel. Since the arches are 48" wide, mark a center point 24" from each side and from one end of the panel (see **fig. 3**). Drill a ¹⁄₁₆" pivot hole through the panel at this point.

2. To make the curves of the arches, cut a 30"-long compass board out of scrap 1 × 8. Remove the blade from your jig saw, and trace the outline of your saw shoe on the compass board, marking where the front edge of the blade fits into the shoe. Beginning at this mark, draw a line parallel to the long edge of the 1 × 8, and continue it to a point 24" away (see **fig. 4**). This will be your pivot point. It is essential that the pivot point and the front edge of the saw blade (once it's reinserted) are in line (equidistant from the side edge of the compass board). After reinserting the jig saw blade, use the electric jig saw to cut out the marked rectangular section, creating a hole inside of which the jig saw shoe fits snugly (see **fig. 5**).

3. Drill a ¹⁄₁₆"-diameter hole at the pivot point, and insert a 1½" or 2" finish nail through the compass board and into the hole in the M.D.O. panel. Use this to cut the arches (see **fig. 6**). As you make the curved cuts, keep in mind that the bottom of the saw blade will have a tendency to angle out away from the center. To prevent this, push the saw slowly along the curve, and keep the motor running at the highest speed. If you have set up your compass board correctly, these curved cuts should be extremely easy to make, and you should achieve a perfect semicircle each time. To cut the inside curve of the arches, make another ¹⁄₁₆" pivot hole 3⅜" from the first hole (see **fig. 4**).

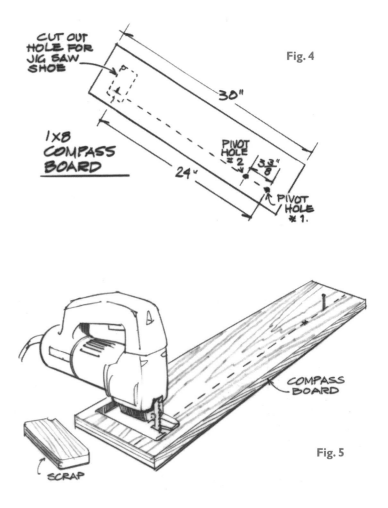

Fig. 4

CUT OUT HOLE FOR JIG SAW SHOE

1×8 COMPASS BOARD

30"

24"

PIVOT HOLE #2

3⅜"

PIVOT HOLE #1

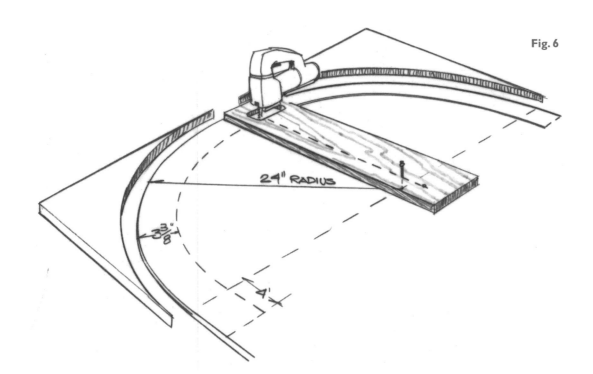

COMPASS BOARD

SCRAP

Fig. 5

Fig. 6

24" RADIUS

3⅜"

4'

Cut off two 11" sections from the waste pieces of M.D.O. plywood — one from the top of the curve and one from the bottom — and glue 1½"-wide coarse (60-grit) sandpaper strips to the curved edges. These sanding blocks will come in handy when sanding the curves, eliminating any chance of flat spots.

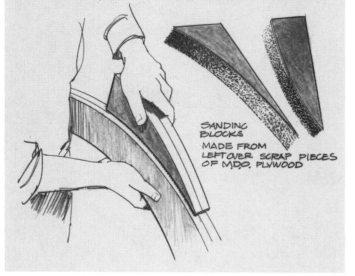

SANDING BLOCKS MADE FROM LEFTOVER SCRAP PIECES OF M.D.O. PLYWOOD

Fig. 7

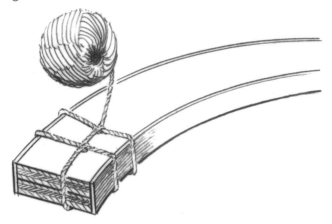

4. Repeat this procedure to cut three more arch pieces. Then stack two pieces on top of each other, making sure they are exactly the same size, and glue them together with waterproof glue. When you are done, you should have two identical 1½"-thick arches.

5. Using a table saw, rip four ³⁄₃₂"-thick strips of clear cedar from the 8'-long 2 × 4. (Set aside the remaining wood for the top slats.) Glue these veneer strips to the edges of the M.D.O. plywood, to hide the end grain. To hold the strips in place while the glue is drying, wrap the arches with heavy hemp twine. Apply waterproof glue to all the surfaces to be glued, and wrap the cord around the strips and the arch. Keep the cord pulled tightly at all times, going back under each previous turn so that the cord can be cinched up securely (see **fig. 7**). There should be no gaps between the strips and the plywood arch. If gaps exist, place wooden shims under the cord.

6. Once the glue has dried, remove the twine and sand the edges smooth, using the sanding blocks. Test fit the ends of the arches to see if they fit into the notches you have made in the posts, then glue them in place with waterproof glue. Make sure both posts are parallel, and screw a temporary 48"-long brace across the bottom to hold them in place. Sink two 2" galvanized deck screws into each joint where the posts meet the arches (see **fig. 8**).

Fig. 8

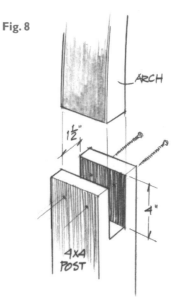

ARCH

1½"

4"

4×4 POST

Capitals and Bases

1. To hide the joints where each arch meets the post, cut four pieces of 1 × 4 clear cedar, at least 5″ long. Bevel each end and temporarily tack them to the post, checking the fit (see **fig. 9**). File and sand until they fit perfectly, and glue them in place. Do the same for the bottom of each post, placing the base pieces exactly 5′ apart, 3″ from the top of the posts.

2. To trim out the top of the capitals, cut two ¾″ × 1″ spacers to a length of 3½″ for each capital, and glue and nail them next to the face of each arch, covering the end grain on the 4 × 4 post. Then cut four 1″ × ¾″ clear cedar trim pieces to a length of 6½″ for each capital. Miter the end of each piece at a 45° angle, and glue and nail them to the top of each capital (see **fig. 9**).

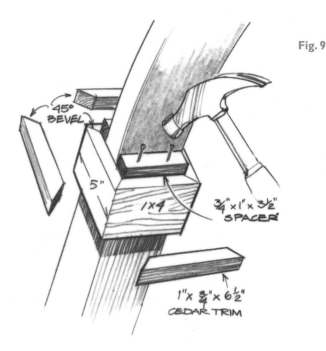

Fig. 9

45° BEVEL

5″

1×4

¾″×1″×3½″ SPACER

1″× ¾″× 6½″ CEDAR TRIM

Crosspieces

1. Cut four crosspieces of clear 2 × 4 cedar, each 19″ long. To attach them to the posts, drill two ⅜″-diameter screw holes, 1½″ deep (see **fig. 10a**). Position the screw holes below the bottom of each capital and ¾″ above each base so that the crosspieces are 50″ apart. Continue drilling the pilot holes, using a 3⁄16″-diameter drill bit, until you come out the other side.

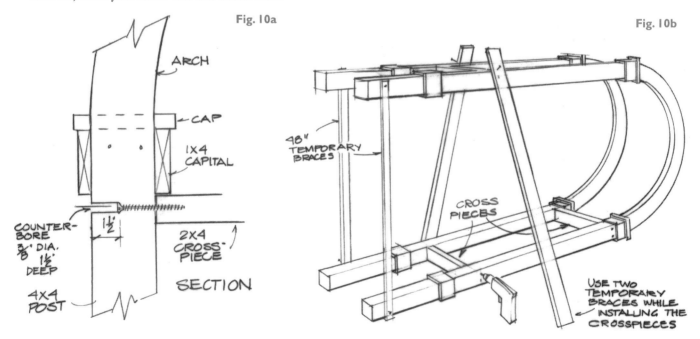

Fig. 10a

ARCH

CAP

1X4 CAPITAL

COUNTER-BORE ⅜″ DIA. 1½″ DEEP

1½″

2X4 CROSS-PIECE

4X4 POST

SECTION

Fig. 10b

48″ TEMPORARY BRACES

CROSS PIECES

USE TWO TEMPORARY BRACES WHILE INSTALLING THE CROSSPIECES

2. Lay the two sets of arches and posts on their sides, facing each other. Glue and screw the crosspieces in place, using 3½" galvanized deck screws. Once you have two crosspieces attached to one pair of posts, turn the structure over and attach the other two crosspieces (see **fig. 10b**).

Lattice

1. Cut four pieces of lattice cap at a length of 19" and four pieces at a length of 47". Cut two pieces of lattice, each 17" × 48" (see **fig. 11**). If you plan on painting this structure, be sure to paint the lattice and support pieces before they are assembled.

2. Glue all the pieces together to form a lattice frame. Fit the lattice frame into the side opening created by the crosspieces and the posts, and screw them in place with 2" galvanized deck screws (see side view, **fig. 1**).

Top Slats

1. Using the wood left over from cutting the veneer strips, rip three 8'-long pieces, each ¾" thick. Cut these into nine pieces, each 27" long.

2. Place the first two pieces 1½" up from the top of the capitals. Align the remaining pieces equidistant from each other, and use 2" deck screws to hold them in place (see **fig. 1**).

Installation

1. To install the rose arbor, dig four 30"-deep holes, using a post hole digger. Fill the bottom of each hole with rocks or bricks (to allow for drainage) until they are 24" deep. To protect the posts, coat the bottom 24" with roofing tar before burying them in the ground.

2. With an assistant, place the arbor legs in the hole and remove the temporary braces. Using a level, check to make sure everything is plumb and level before backfilling, and tamp the dirt down with a 2 × 4 as you go.

Fig. 11

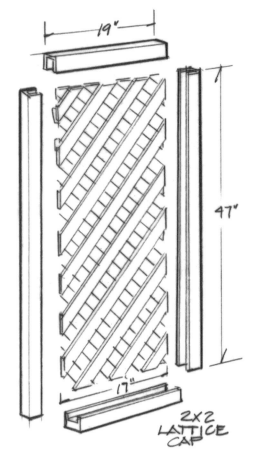

19"

47"

17"

2X2 LATTICE CAP

Pergola

David built this pergola for Helena Cresci, a floral designer, whose vision was to create a garden room reminiscent of southern France or Italy. The columns were salvaged from a friends' home that was being renovated, then scraped down to bare wood, sanded until smooth, and covered with several coats of polyurethane. The clear coating revealed the inherent blemishes and paint-speckle residue left on the columns, giving them an antique look. She and David completed the design together, placing the pergola in the back of the garden, defining the space without actually enclosing it.

The pergola's visual appeal is in the repetition of the roof elements, which create a rhythm of light and dark as you pass under them. Its charm lies in the fact that it appears to be a strong architectural element with classical details, yet it really serves no purpose except to show off climbing roses or clematis, and therefore might be considered a "folly" by some. For Helena, it is a cool spot where she can relax and enjoy a glass of wine underneath an arbor of grapes.

Materials Needed

Qty.	Size	Description	Location or Use
Columns			
2	12'	4 x 4 #2 cedar or P.T. posts	inner post
6	14'	1 x 8 cedar	columns
6	14'	1 x 6 cedar	columns
1	6'	2 x 12 clear pine	capital
2	12'	1⅛" x 1⅝" solid crown	capital
2	12'	1¹¹⁄₁₆" x 1⅛" nose cove molding	capital
2	12'	⅞" x 1¹¹⁄₁₆" cove molding	base
2	12'	1 x 8 pine	base
8	80-lb. bag	concrete mix	post holes
6	1¼"	aluminum vents	columns
1 lb.	3"	galvanized deck screws	columns
Horizontal top pieces			
4	16'	2 x 8 cedar	beams
14	10'	2 x 6 cedar	rafters
1	12'	6 x 6 cedar	inner posts

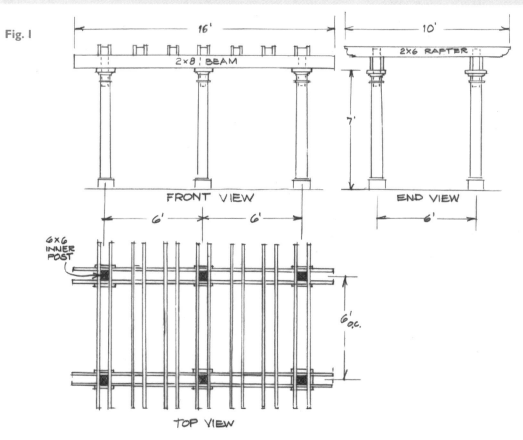

Fig. 1

FRONT VIEW   END VIEW

TOP VIEW

Installing Columns

A column is nothing more than four long boards joined together, with molding attached at the top and bottom. If you are going to paint your columns, use ordinary pine lumber. However, if you are going to let them weather gray, use cedar, redwood, or cypress. In either case, make sure to coat the bottom (even the insides) with a water sealer. A miter box is useful for making the molding cuts, but a hand saw can do the job as well.

Most columns, whether store bought, homemade, or salvaged, have a hollow core, which will enable you to place the column over a pressure-treated post embedded in the ground. By using a P.T. post with dimensions smaller than the interior dimensions of the column, you can make any final adjustments before cementing the column in place.

1. Start by locating the six post locations (see Setting Corner Markers on page 10 and **fig. 1**) and digging a 30"-deep hole for each post. Cut six 4 × 4 posts long enough so that 12" to 16" will protrude above the ground. Bury and align the posts so they are plumb, square, and the correct distance apart (6' on center). Backfill with soil. Pour a 3"- to 4"-thick concrete collar around the base of each post just below the ground level (see section column base, **fig. 2**).

2. Once the concrete has hardened, set the columns over the 4 × 4 inner posts, and secure them with four 1 × 2 temporary support braces (see **fig. 3**). Drill a 1⅜" vent hole through the side of the column, slightly above where the inside post is, and place a removable vent cap in the hole. Do not fill the columns with cement yet (see **fig. 2**).

3. Insert a 6 × 6 post inside the top of each column, allowing it to protrude 12" above the top. Attach each column securely to its inner post with a screw on each side of the column. Join the 2 × 8 horizontal beams to the columns by lifting them in place and screwing them to the 6 × 6 protruding inner post, using three 3" galvanized deck screws on each side. Shape the rafter tails as described below (see **fig. 4**), and

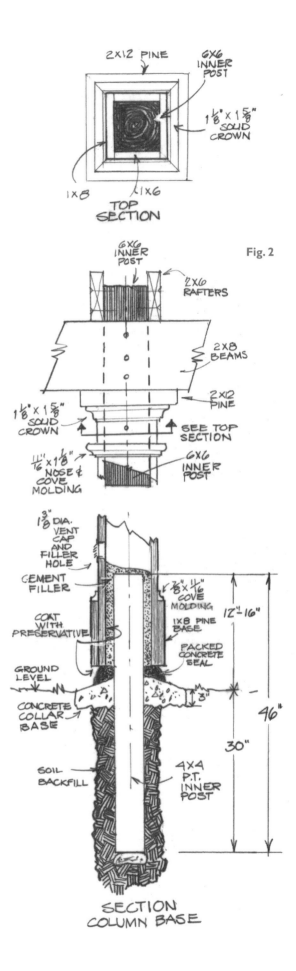

2×12 PINE
6×6 INNER POST
1⅛" × 1⅝" SOLID CROWN
1×8
1×6
TOP SECTION

Fig. 2
6×6 INNER POST
2×6 RAFTERS
2×8 BEAMS
2×12 PINE
1⅛" × 1⅝" SOLID CROWN
SEE TOP SECTION
⁷⁄₁₆" × 1⅛" NOSE & COVE MOLDING
6×6 INNER POST

1⅜" DIA. VENT CAP AND FILLER HOLE
CEMENT FILLER
COAT WITH PRESERVATIVE
GROUND LEVEL
CONCRETE COLLAR BASE
SOIL BACKFILL
⅞" × ⁷⁄₁₆" COVE MOLDING
1×8 PINE BASE
PACKED CONCRETE SEAL
12"–16"
3"
46"
30"
4×4 P.T. INNER POST

SECTION COLUMN BASE

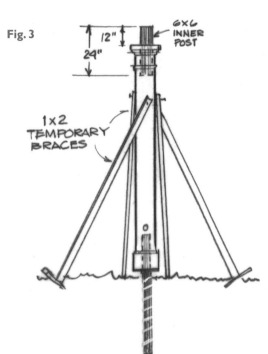

Fig. 3

6×6 INNER POST

12"

24"

1×2 TEMPORARY BRACES

screw them to the 6 × 6 inner post, so that they are perpendicular to the cedar beams. The column, beam, and rafters are now all securely locked together (see **fig. 2**).

4. Pack the base of the column with concrete and allow it to harden. Remove the vent cap, and pour in a wet mixture of cement to fill the empty space between the inner post and the column. After the cement has hardened, remove the braces (see **fig. 2**).

Rafter Tails

There are several different ways in which the tails, or ends, of the 2 × 6 rafters can be cut to make a more decorative appearance. Choose a pattern from those shown below or make your own design. Make a template from a piece of cardboard and trace it onto both ends of each 2 × 6. Use an electric jig saw to cut out all the pieces, and sand them smooth. This is time consuming, but it will add a decorative finished look to the overall design of the columns (see **fig. 4**).

Fig. 4

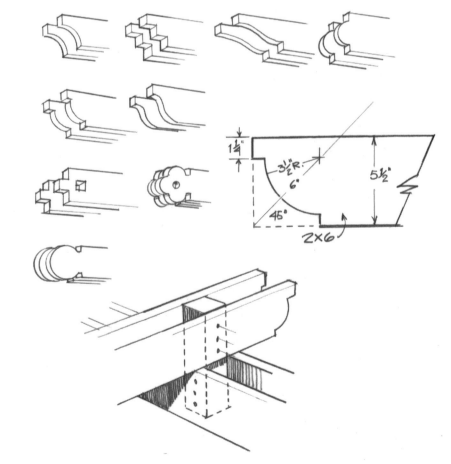

Bridge with Bamboo Arbor

The three elements of this design — a bridge, a bench, and an arbor — are combined to create a cool spot to sit and relax in between garden chores. The bridge, which can be built over a pond, brook, or wetland area, serves to connect one garden room to another. The patterns made by the sun falling through the bamboo arbor provide just enough soft light to warm the bench.

Materials Needed

Qty.	Size	Description	Location or Use
4	10'	salvaged telephone poles	main support
2	8'	salvaged telephone poles	deck support
4	6'6"	salvaged telephone poles	railing poles
2	8'	2 × 8 P.T. lumber	side cross beams
6	4'	2 × 8 P.T. lumber	ramp frame
5	7'	2 × 8 P.T. lumber	floor joists
16	4'	2 × 8 P.T. lumber or wood slabs	ramps
12	7'	2 × 8 P.T. lumber or wood slabs	deck
2	7'	3 × 8 fir	cross beams
4	2'	2 × 8 fir	knee braces
1	8'	2 × 8 fir	back crosstie
6	7'	4 × 6 fir	rafters
2	5'	2 × 2 fir	rafter ties
3	7'	2½" diameter fresh saplings	decorative arches
14	7'	2"-diameter bamboo	roof
1	7'	4 × 4 cedar	ridgepole
2	7'	3½"-diameter cedar logs	seat
4	30"	3½"-diameter cedar logs	seat
1	8'	2½"-diameter fresh sapling	seat arch
1	6'	1¼"-diameter fresh sapling	smaller seat arch
9	30"	2½"-diameter fresh saplings	seat back
26	24"	2½"-diameter fresh saplings	seat
2	12"	3½"-diameter cedar logs	vertical support logs
30	3½"	galvanized deck screws	rafters
1	6'	1⅛"-diameter hemp rope	
1	12' × 16'	heavy-duty black poly. pond liner	

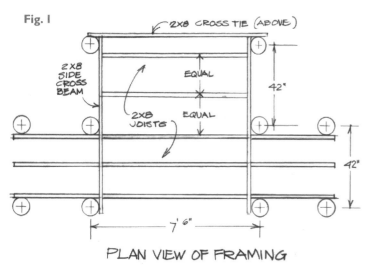

Fig. 1

PLAN VIEW OF FRAMING

Bridge and Bench

1. Cut and embed four 10'-long salvaged telephone poles. Bury them 4' in the ground to make a 3½' × 7'6" rectangle. To provide a railing post and support for the front deck, embed two 7'-long poles, 3'6" in front of the first four poles, so that the tops emerge 4' out of the ground. Provide a pair of 30"-high, 5'-long poles at the bottom ends of the ramp to support the rope railing. After making sure the poles are plumb, backfill with soil, compacting as you fill. If necessary, place concrete around

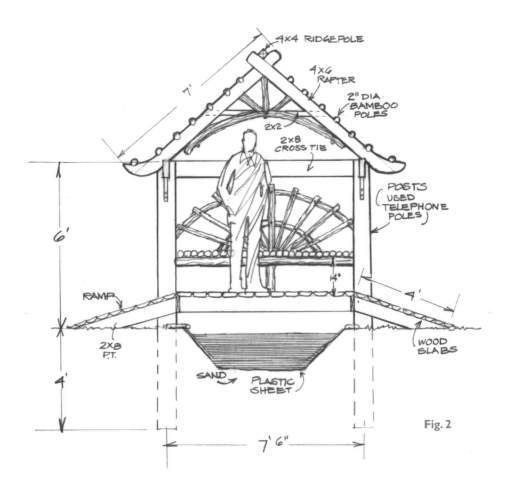

4×4 RIDGEPOLE

4×6 RAFTER

2" DIA. BAMBOO POLES

2×2

2×8 CROSS TIE

POSTS (USED TELEPHONE POLES)

7'

6'

4"

4'

RAMP

2×8 P.T.

SAND

PLASTIC SHEET

WOOD SLABS

7' 6"

Fig. 2

the poles where they emerge from the ground, to make sure they will not move.

2. Build the two ramps and the floor by bolting pressure-treated 2 × 8s to the inside of the posts, securing them with two ½" × 4" galvanized lag bolts at each joint. Frame the ramps using six 4'-long P.T. 2 × 8s. To support the floor boards, cut five 2 × 8 floor joists to fit between the 2 × 8 side cross beams (see **figs. 1 and 6**). Cover the ramp frame and deck with wood slabs, which can often be found discarded at saw mills (see **fig. 2**). If no saw mills are available, substitute 2 × 8 P.T. lumber.

3. To frame the top, cut two pieces of 3 × 8 fir at a length of 7', and shape the ends (see **figs. 3 and 4**). Using a chain saw, cut a notch in the tops of the four main posts to accept the 3 × 8 upper cross beams. Bore two 1"-diameter holes through the ends of the posts. Join the beams to the posts by hammering pegs through the holes. Use 1"-diameter oak pegs made from sticks. Remove the bark and whittle them down until they fit (see **fig. 4**).

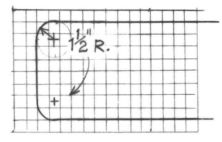

1½" R.

Fig. 3

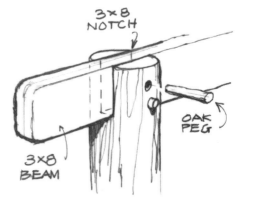

3×8 NOTCH

3×8 BEAM

OAK PEG

Fig. 4

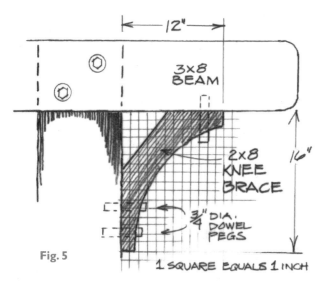

Fig. 5

12"

3×8 BEAM

2×8 KNEE BRACE

16"

3/4" DIA. DOWEL PEGS

1 SQUARE EQUALS 1 INCH

4. Cut knee braces from 2 × 8 fir following the profile shown in **fig. 5,** and peg them to the underside of the upper cross beams and to the posts.

5. Cut an 8'-long piece of 2 × 8 for the back crosstie, and screw it to the two rear posts, using two ½" × 4" lag bolts at each joint (see **figs. 2 and 6**).

6. To build the roof trusses, cut six pieces of 4 × 6 fir, each 7' long. Lay the pieces on the ground and cross the tops so that 6" extends beyond where they cross. Mark and cut notches so the two pieces fit together flush (see **fig. 7**). Construct the tops and tailends as shown in **figs. 7 and 8**, and glue and peg the lap joints together. To keep the rafters from spreading, screw a 2 × 2 rafter-tie to the rafters, positioned 42" down from the top of each rafter (see **figs. 7 and 8**). Temporarily set the rafters in place (36" on center), and mark where the bird's mouth (notches) should go (see **fig. 9**). Remove the rafters and cut the notches. Reposition the rafters and toenail them to the 3 × 8 side beams.

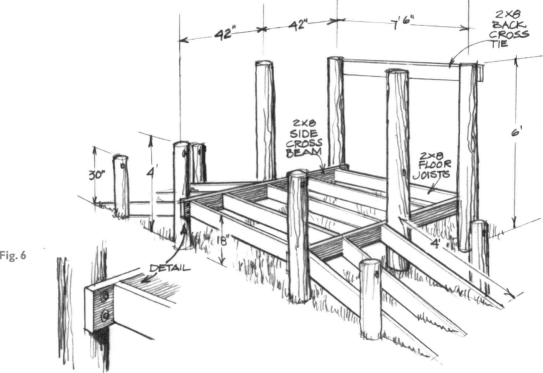

Fig. 6

42" 42" 7'6"

2×8 BACK CROSS TIE

6'

2×8 SIDE CROSS BEAM

2×8 FLOOR JOISTS

30" 4'

18"

DETAIL

4'

7. Drill 1¼"-diameter holes near the top of the front posts. String 1⅛"-diameter rope through the holes and knot the ends.

8. From the woods find three fresh, 7'-long, 2½"-diameter saplings. Remove the bark with a spoke shave, and bend two of them into an arch to fit inside the two rafters. Attach the saplings to the rafters and the 2 × 2, using 3½"-long galvanized screws. A sapling is not required in the middle pair of rafters. Cut six short pieces of 2½"-diameter peeled saplings, three pieces to fit above each arch. Toenail them to the arches and rafters (see **fig. 8**).

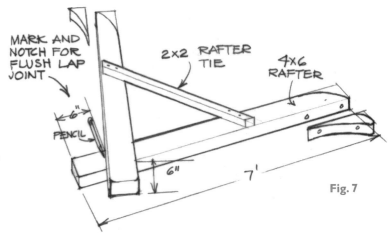

Fig. 7

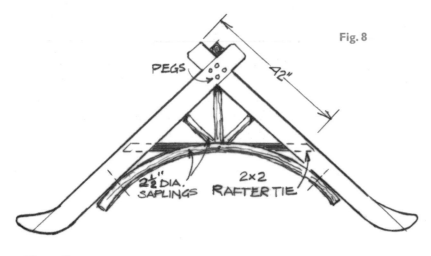

Fig. 8

Roof

1. Cut fourteen 2"-diameter bamboo poles, each 7' long. Space them 10" apart along the rafters. Cut ¾"-deep circular notches for the bamboo to rest on the rafters (see **fig. 9**). Peg the bamboo to the rafters, using ½"-diameter wood pegs.

2. For the ridgepole, cut a 7'-long piece of 4 × 4 cedar, and screw it to the saddle created by the crossed rafters.

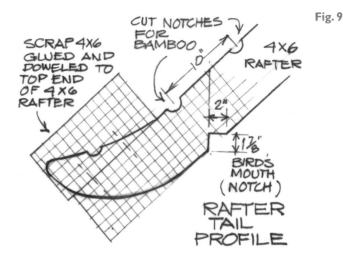

Fig. 9

Seat

1. To make the frame for the seat, cut two 3½"-diameter logs at a length of 7', and cut four 3½"-diameter logs at a length of 30". Join the logs to the posts and to each other by cutting concave curves out of the ends to match the outside curves of the posts, and toenail them in place.

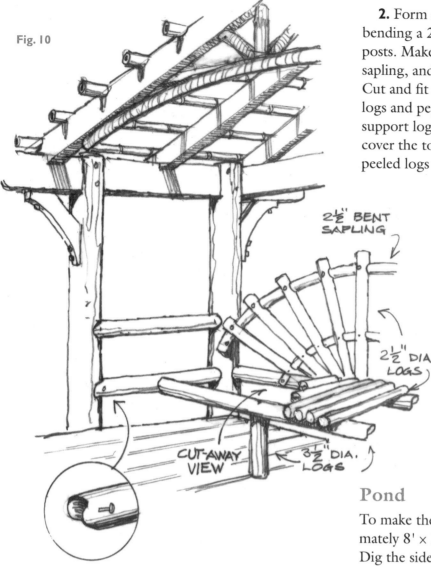

Fig. 10

2. Form an arch for the back of the seat by bending a 2½" sapling to fit between the rear posts. Make a smaller arch out of 1¼"-diameter sapling, and join it to the back of the bench. Cut and fit nine radial pieces of peeled 2½" logs and peg them to the arches. Add a vertical support log under the center of the bench, and cover the top of the bench with 2½"-diameter peeled logs nailed to the bench (see **fig. 10**).

2½" BENT SAPLING

2½" DIA LOGS

CUT-AWAY VIEW

3½" DIA. LOGS

Pond

To make the pond, excavate an area approximately 8' × 12' and at a depth of 18" to 24". Dig the sides at a 45° angle so they will not cave in. Make sure that the edge of the pond is level, then cover the sides and bottom of the pond with moist sand. Trim the overlapping plastic to within 8" of the pool edge, and secure with stones (see **fig. 11**).

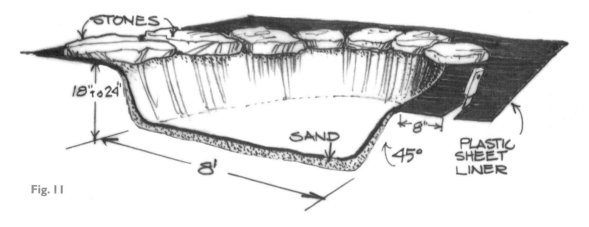

STONES

18" to 24"

SAND

8"

8'

45°

PLASTIC SHEET LINER

Fig. 11

Covered Doorway

Part of the appeal of this ornamental gate entrance is the contrast between its diminutive height and the sturdy, oversized posts supporting it. One must stoop slightly to pass under the low roof, hoping perhaps to find a child's fantasy garden on the other side of the gate. The space between the roof and the pickets creates a perfect frame for a vegetable or cutting garden, or even an open field.

Qty.	Size	Description	Location or Use
2	8'	8' × 8' P.T. lumber	posts
1	6'	8' × 8' P.T. lumber	cross supports
1	6'	4 × 6 fir	knee braces
1	10'	6 × 6 fir	lintels
2	8'	2 × 4 fir	rafters
1	6'	2 × 6 fir	ridgepole
6	12'	1 × 6 #2 pine	roof sheathing
1 bundle	18"	hand-split cedar shakes	roof
2	10"	½"-diameter lag screws	cross-support fasteners
4	8"	½"-diameter lag screws	beams

Fig. 1

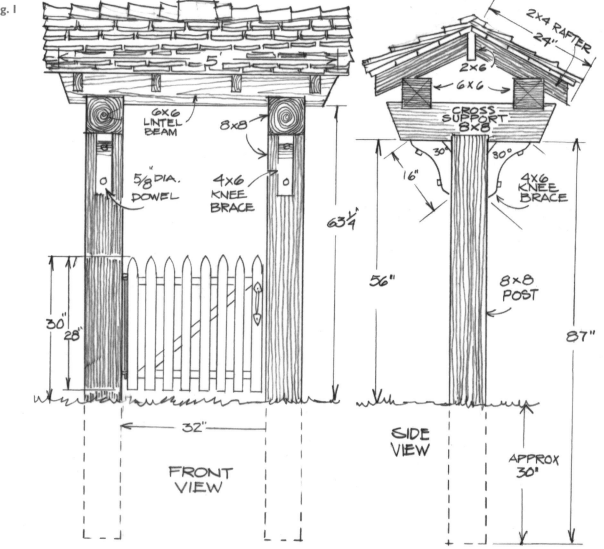

1. Begin by cutting the 8' × 8' posts and cross-supports to length: two pieces 7' long and two pieces 3' long (see **fig. 2**). Cut off the ends of the cross-supports at 30° angles. Make a 1"-deep notch in the bottom side of the cross-supports to accept the posts (see **fig. 3**).

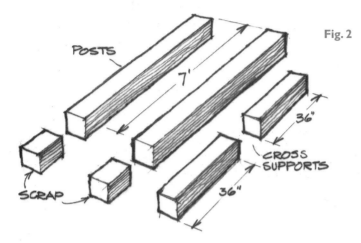

Fig. 2

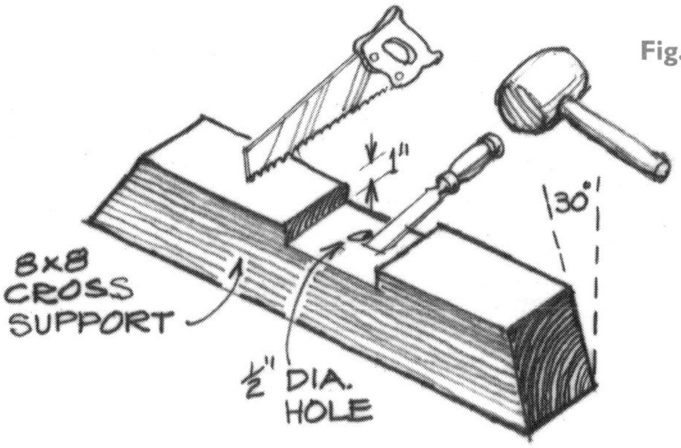

POSTS

7'

36"

36"

SCRAP

CROSS SUPPORTS

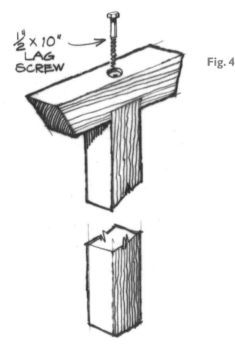

Fig. 3

8×8 CROSS SUPPORT

1"

30°

½" DIA. HOLE

2. Bore a ½"-diameter hole through the center of the notch, and screw the cross-supports to the posts, using a 10"-long lag screw. Recess the head of the screw 1½" (see **fig. 4**).

3. Bury the bottoms of the posts 30" in the ground, leaving 56" extending above ground. Use scrap lumber to temporarily brace the posts after making sure they are plumb and square with each other then backfill with concrete.

4. Cut two lintel beams from 6 × 6 lumber, each 5' long. Cut the ends off at 30° angles. Rest them on the cross-supports, and mark where they meet. Cut 1"-deep notches, and screw the lintel beams to the cross-supports, using ½" × 8" lag screws recessed 1½" in from the top (see **fig. 5**).

½" × 10" LAG SCREW

Fig. 4

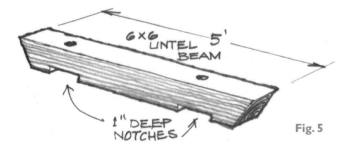

6×6 LINTEL BEAM 5'

1" DEEP NOTCHES

Fig. 5

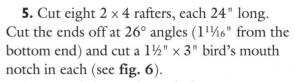

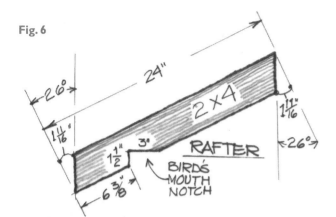

Fig. 6

5. Cut eight 2 × 4 rafters, each 24" long. Cut the ends off at 26° angles (1¹¹⁄₁₆" from the bottom end) and cut a 1½" × 3" bird's mouth notch in each (see **fig. 6**).

6. Cut a 5'-long ridge pole from a 2 × 6. Toenail the rafters to the ridgepole and lintels approximately 17" apart (see **fig. 7**).

7. To build the roof, cut eight 1 × 6 boards, each 67½" long, and nail them to the rafters. Cover the boards with clay tiles or hand-split cedar shakes. Stagger the shakes so that the joints do not line up, and double the first layer (see **fig. 8**).

8. To cover the top ridge, cut shakes 3½" wide, and weave them across the top, perpendicular to the shakes on the main part of the roof (see **fig. 9**).

Fig. 7

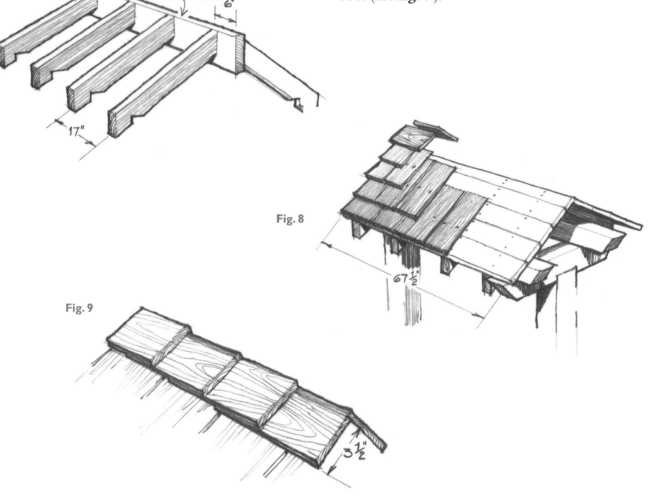

Fig. 8

Fig. 9

9. To support the cross supports, cut four 4 × 6 knee braces, each 16" long (see **fig. 10**). The curves can best be cut using a band saw, but if you don't have access to a band saw, you can use an electric jig saw with a 5" blade. Join the knee braces to the cross supports and the posts, using ⅝"-diameter wood pegs driven through the braces and into the post.

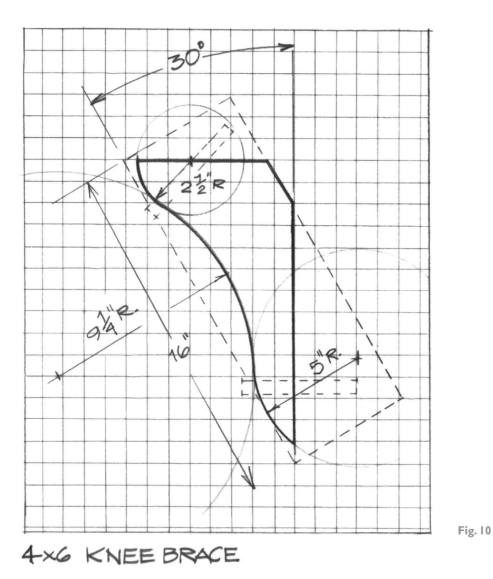

Fig. 10

4×6 KNEE BRACE

Folly/Gate Post

These ornate posts can be used as gate posts or planted singly in a remote part of your garden as a folly. One friend of ours, a gentleman farmer, made one and planted it in his vegetable garden. Although it serves no useful purpose, he is justifiably proud of it and receives many compliments from friends and neighbors. We built a similar post at the entrance to a country estate. The construction is fairly easy if one has a table saw, but it can also be built using hand tools, substituting cove moldings for the 45° bevel cuts in the sides of the post. The ball at the top can be bought from most lumberyards or special ordered.

Like most large posts, this one is hollow and fits over a pressure-treated post that has been cemented into the ground. Make sure the bottom of the decorative post is a few inches above the ground to allow for ventilation, or provide ½"-diameter weep holes in an inconspicuous spot.

Qty.	Size	Description	Location or Use
4	10'	1 × 4 clear pine	post corners
1	10'	1 × 6 clear pine	top and bottom trim
1	5'	⅞" × ⅞" cove molding	top trim
1	⅜" × 5"	hanger bolt	finial
1	4' × 8'	¾" M.D.O. plywood*	sides and top
1	8"-diameter	wood	finial ball
1	8" × 8"	P.T. post (cut to suit)	
1 box	2"	galvanized finishing nails	
1 box	2"	galvanized deck screws	
1	twin tube	epoxy resin	

*We recommend that you use ¾"-thick M.D.O. (medium density overlay), plywood for this project, since it is highly resistant to weather and holds paint well. The materials listed here are for a single post.

1. From a 4 × 8 panel of ¾" M.D.O., cut a piece 5' long. Cut this piece into four 11¼"-wide pieces. Save the remaining panel of plywood for the top of the folly (see **fig. 1**).

2. Glue and nail the plywood pieces together, using 2" finishing nails, to form a 12" square, 5' tall box (see **fig. 2**).

3. Using a table saw, rip a 45° bevel on one edge of the 1 × 6 board. To make the top and bottom trim, cut eight pieces, each 13½" long. Bevel cut the ends at 45° (see **fig. 3**).

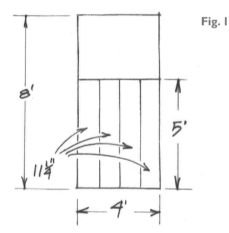

Fig. 1

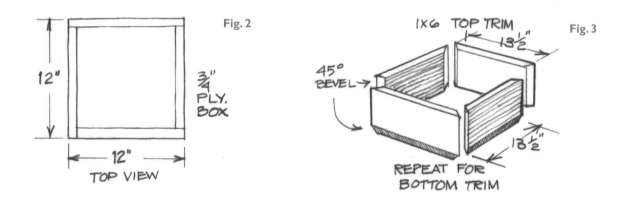

Fig. 2

Fig. 3

4. Glue and nail the top and bottom trim to the box, using 2"-long galvanized finishing nails **(see fig. 4).**

5. Rip a 45° bevel along both edges of eight 1 × 4 boards. Carefully measure and cut the ends at 45° bevels to fit between the top and bottom 1 × 6 beveled trim (see **fig. 5**).

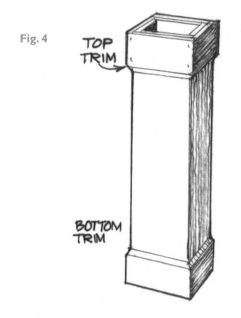

Fig. 4

TOP TRIM

BOTTOM TRIM

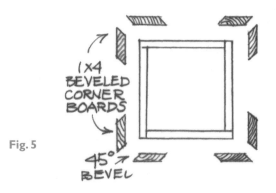

Fig. 5

1×4 BEVELED CORNER BOARDS

45° BEVEL

6. To make the ledge at the top of the post, cut four 17"-long pieces of clear 2 × 4. Miter the ends at 45° angles and glue them together to form a square (see **fig. 6**). Mitered corners invariably start to spread apart over time. To help prevent this, screw 3"-long #6 screws at right angles to each other into each corner. Make sure to offset them a little so they don't meet inside the wood (see **fig. 7**).

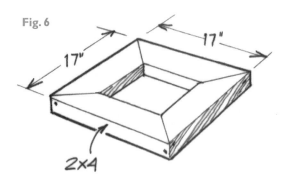

Fig. 6

17"

17"

2×4

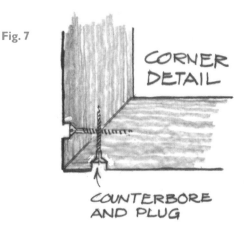

Fig. 7

CORNER DETAIL

COUNTERBORE AND PLUG

7. To make a base for the wooden ball, cut three square pieces out of leftover ¾" M.D.O. plywood: one 8" × 8", one 13" × 13", and one 15" × 15". Sand and coat the edges with epoxy resin to prevent them from delaminating. Glue and nail the three pieces to the 2 × 4 ledge (see **fig. 8**).

8. Drill a ⅜" hole in the center of the top square, and use a ⅜" × 5" hanger screw to attach the ball to the post (see **fig. 9**).

9. Measure and cut four pieces of cove molding, and nail them to fit under the ledge pieces.

10. To install the decorative post, bury the bottom end of an 8' × 8' post 30" in the ground. Cut the top off so that 4½' protrude above the ground. If the post is to be used to hang a gate, backfill around it with concrete; otherwise, use a 2 × 4 to tamp down the backfill soil. Make sure the post is plumb and vertical on all sides. Stand on a stepladder while you drop the decorative post over the 8' × 8' interior post. Wedge the decorative post up with temporary blocks of wood, and attach the outside post to the inside post on two sides, using 2" galvanized screws (see **fig. 10**).

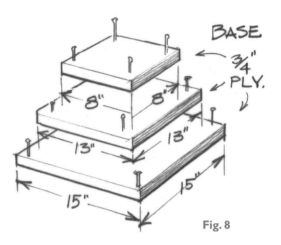

BASE
¾" PLY.
8" 8"
13" 13"
15" 15"

Fig. 8

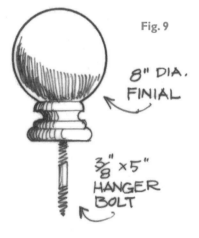

Fig. 9

8" DIA. FINIAL

⅜" × 5" HANGER BOLT

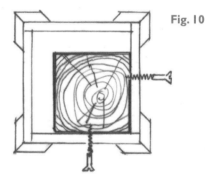

Fig. 10

Picket Gate

Nothing is more American than a white picket fence and gate. Mark Twain described how Tom Sawyer walked along a picket fence with a stick, clicking the fence as he went along. This simple gate should take only a morning to build. You can buy ready-cut pickets if you like. Otherwise, rip and cut them from a 10'-long 1 × 8. Before ordering your lumber, consider what might pass through the gate (lawn mower, garden cart, or even a tractor) and how wide you need to make it. If 36" is not wide enough, you may need to order more materials and adapt the directions accordingly.

Qty.	Size	Description	Location or Use
2	6'	4 × 4 clear cedar	posts
2	4' × 4'	post caps	posts
1	10'	1 × 8	pickets
1	10'	1 × 4	diagonal and cross braces
1 lb.	1½"	galvanized finishing nails	diagonal and cross braces
2 bags		concrete	base
1 pair		hinges	
1		gate latch	
2		handles	
1 qt.		exterior paint	
1 can		wood putty	

Cutting the Pickets

1. Rip a 10'-long 1 × 8 into three equal-sized pieces of wood. Cut three 40"-long pickets from each piece, making a total of nine pickets. Place the pickets on a flat work surface spaced evenly apart (approximately 2"), and line up the bottoms. Temporarily nail or clamp the first end picket to the work surface so it won't move. Measure 35½" from the outside of the first picket, and temporarily nail down the last picket. Use a framing square to make sure the pickets line up parallel with one another (see **fig. 1**). Make sure the remaining pickets are spaced equidistant apart.

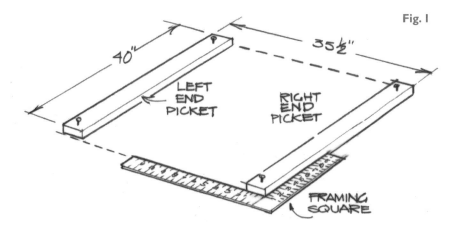

Fig. 1

40"

35½"

LEFT END PICKET

RIGHT END PICKET

FRAMING SQUARE

2. Cut two cross braces (cleats), both to a length of 35". Glue and nail the cross braces to the pickets, 3" up from the bottom and 2½" down from the top of the gate (see **fig. 2**).

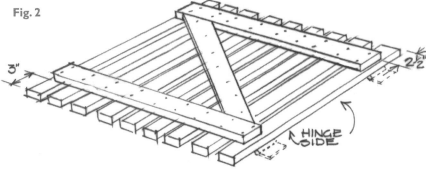

Fig. 2

3"

2½"

HINGE SIDE

Use 1½" finishing nails, and slant each nail so that it won't extend out the other side of the wood. This will also help the nails to hold better. Set the nails a little below the surface, using a nail set, and fill with wood putty (see **fig. 3**).

3. Mark where the diagonal brace will meet the two cross braces, and cut the diagonal to fit. Glue and nail the brace to the top cross brace on the latch side and the bottom cross brace on the hinge side (see **fig. 4**), slanting the nails in the same manner. Round off all exposed edges of wood, using #80 sandpaper. This is an important step because paint does not adhere well to sharp edges, allowing water to penetrate the wood and causing the paint to peel as a result.

4. Remove the temporary nails from the end pickets.

Installation

1. Cut two 6'-long posts out of 4 × 4 clear cedar. Dig two holes, 24" deep, 39½" from center to center. Position the posts in the holes, making sure that they are plumb and that the tops of the posts are square and level with each other.

2. Screw one side of each hinge to the gate. Prop up the gate next to the post, allowing ¼" clearance on each side, and screw the other half of each hinge to the post. Attach the gate handles and latch. Nail temporary braces to hold the posts in place, and backfill each post hole with concrete.

Fig. 3

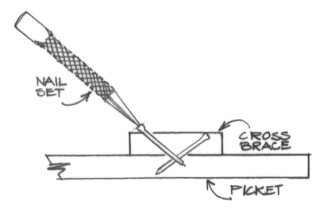

NAIL SET

CROSS BRACE

PICKET

Fig. 4

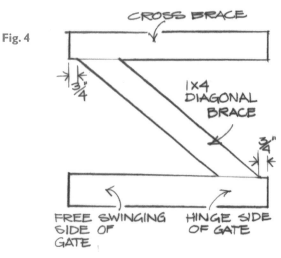

CROSS BRACE

¾

1×4 DIAGONAL BRACE

¾

FREE SWINGING SIDE OF GATE

HINGE SIDE OF GATE

Arched Gate

What starts out to be an old-fashioned, simple gate to construct becomes slightly more formal and elegant with the addition of a graceful arch. Looking through the space above the swinging gate and below the arch should frame a garden view and invite a guest to enter another outdoor area. We used our gate to access a garden-fringed swimming pool and trained miniature roses to climb up the sides of the white-painted pickets. The gate creates a sense of privacy, while at the same time opening the door to another garden room.

Fig. 1

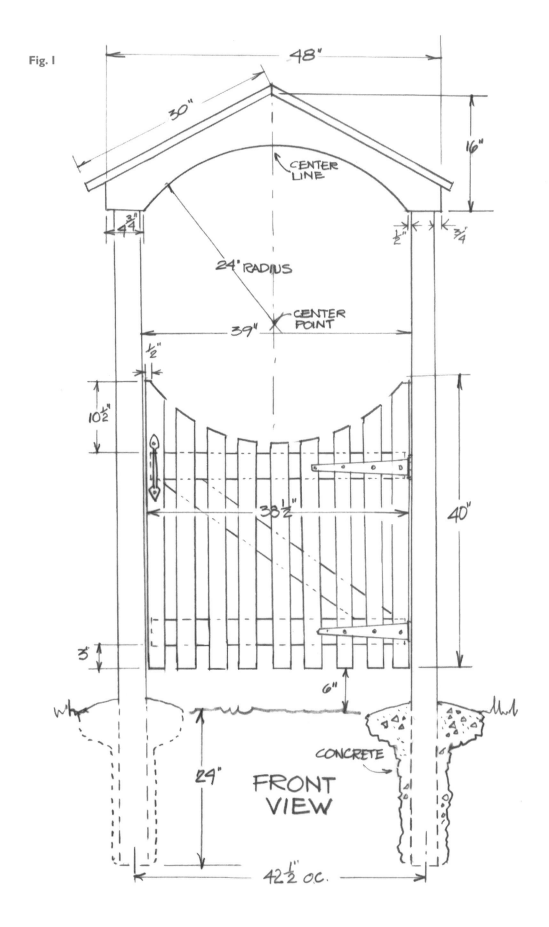

48"

30"

16"

CENTER
LINE

3/4"

1/2"

3/4"

24" RADIUS

CENTER
POINT

39"

1/2"

10 1/2"

38 1/2"

40"

3"

6"

CONCRETE

29"

FRONT
VIEW

42 1/2" O.C.

Qty.	Size	Description	Location or Use
½" sheet	4' × 4'	¾" M.D.O. plywood	arches
2	8'	4 × 4 clear cedar	posts
1	6'	1 × 6 #2 pine	roof
1	10'	1 × 4 #2 pine	2 cross braces, 1 diag. brace
1	10'	1 × 8 #2 pine	pickets
1 pair		galvanized self-closing hinges	
or			
1 pair	8"-long	strap hinges	
1		gate latch	
1 box	2"	galvanized deck screws	
1 box	1¼"	galvanized finishing nails	
1 qt.		epoxy and hardener	
1	8 oz.	Titebond II waterproof glue	
1	40 lbs.	concrete dry mix (sacrete)	

Building the Arches

1. Draw a line down the center of a ¾"-thick M.D.O. (medium density overlay) plywood panel. Measure and make a mark 16" down from the top of each side. Make a second mark 3½" down from each of the first marks. Using a square, measure in 4¾" from this second set of points and make a mark. Use these points to draw two 24"-radius arcs, intersecting at a point on the centerline. This will be your center point to draw the arc. Do this by drilling a hole in a 28"-long piece of thin wood that is wide enough for a pencil point to poke through. Hammer a small nail in the other end of the stick, exactly 24" from the center of the pencil point hole. Place the nail on the center-line point and draw a 24" arc (see **fig. 2**).

2. Using an electric jig saw, cut out the plywood arches (see **fig. 3**). Use a rough grade of sandpaper to remove any irregularities in the curve, and finish with progressively less coarse sandpaper until the curve is perfect. Using the cut-out piece as a template, make a second, identical arch.

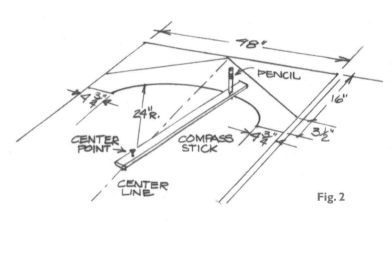

Fig. 2

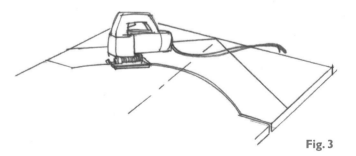

Fig. 3

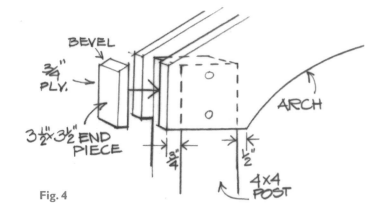

Fig. 4

3. Place two 8'-long pieces of 4 × 4 clear cedar flat on the ground so they are parallel and 39" apart. Countersink and screw the two arches to the tops of the 4 × 4 posts. The arches should overlap the posts by ¾" on the outside and ½" on the inside.

4. Cut two 3½" × 3½" pieces of plywood to fit between the arches against the post, and glue and nail them in place. Before attaching the end pieces, bevel the top of each one to match the angle at the top of the arch (see **fig. 4**).

5. Cut two 1 × 6 roof pieces to a length of 30", and bevel the ends so they fit together at the top (see **fig. 5**). Glue and nail these roof pieces to the top of the plywood arches. Cover all exposed edges with two coats of epoxy and sand smooth.

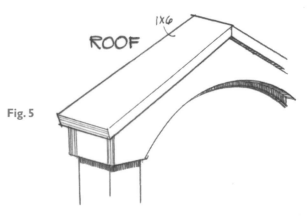

Fig. 5

6. To prevent the posts from getting out of alignment, screw a scrap piece of lumber across them, 24" up from the bottom (see **fig. 6**).

Pickets

1. Follow the instructions for the Picket Gate on page 76, cutting nine 40"-long pickets. Make the gate 38½" wide, which allows ¼" clearance between the gate and the posts. Cut the cross braces at a length of 38", and attach the top cross brace 10½" down from the top of the pickets.

2. Use the arch as a template to reproduce an identical curve at the top of the picket gate. Place it over the top of the pickets and trace

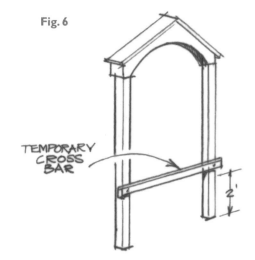

Fig. 6

the curve with a pencil (see **fig. 7**). Cut out the curve, using an electric jig saw. Trim the sharp pointed edges of the two outermost pickets so that they measure ½" across the top (see **fig. 8**). Sand the wood using #80 and #120 grit sandpaper, and paint all the surfaces with three coats of exterior semigloss paint.

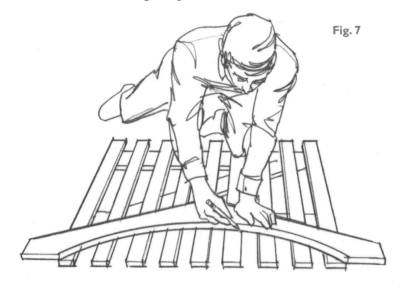

Fig. 7

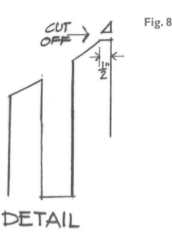

Fig. 8

CUT OFF →

½"

DETAIL

3. Attach the gate to one of the posts. We used spring-loaded, self-closing hinges because our gate was installed around a pool. However, strap hinges also work well and look more traditional with a picket gate. We attached a typical gate latch that snaps shut and can be padlocked if necessary.

Installation

To install the gate, dig two 24"-deep post holes, using the assembled gate, posts, and arch as a guide. Lift the gate into place, and level it by placing blocks under the temporary crosspiece (see **fig. 9**). Once it is plumb and level, support it with temporary braces. Backfill the holes with concrete to make sure the gate won't get out of alignment later on. Allow the concrete to cure for several days before removing the temporary braces.

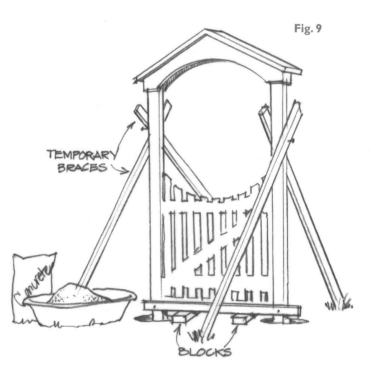

Fig. 9

TEMPORARY BRACES

BLOCKS

Garden Shelters

A shelter — A retreat, sanctuary, refuge from the elements.

—Random House Dictionary

Gardener's Retreat

Because of its simplicity, this classic garden house can be used as a potting shed or be converted into an artist's studio or a children's playhouse. It is especially attractive stained or painted white or a dark Charleston green. Create a curving pebbled path leading up to the front door, and end it with a nice piece of slate or bluestone.

When picking a shed site on your property, make sure that it conforms to the building code, and obtain a building permit for an accessory structure from the building department. Look for a level spot, free from roots and stones, that is easily accessible to your garden.

Qty.	Size	Description	Location or Use
Floor			
2	10'	2 x 6 P.T. lumber	floor
1	14'	2 x 6 P.T. lumber	floor
2	14'	2 x 6 P.T. lumber	floor joists
varies	4' x 8' x 16'	solid concrete blocks	base
varies		slate shims	base
2	4' x 8'	¾" exterior plywood	floor
Walls			
6	10'	2 x 4 construction fir	front and back plates
3	14'	2 x 4 construction fir	end plates
10	12'	2 x 4 construction fir	studs
3	12'	2 x 4 construction fir	horizontal nailers and window framing
384 lin. ft.	1 x 8	T&G #2 pine	siding
Roof			
5	10'	2 x 4 #2 construction fir	rafters
1	4' x 4' sheet	½" plywood	gussets
1	10'	1 x 2	ridgepole
1 roll	6" wide	insect screening	eaves
Roof Trim			
2	10'	1 x 4 #2 pine	fascia boards
2	10'	1 x 4 #2 pine	gable trim
2	12'	1¹⁄₁₆" x 1⅜" solid crown	roof molding
2	10'	1¹⁄₁₆" x 1⅜" solid crown	roof molding
2	10'	1 x 6	eave boards
22	10'	1 x 4	spaced sheathing
Roofing			
5 bundles	18"	premium red-cedar shingles	roofing
2	12'	1 x 4 #2 cedar	ridge trim
Windows			
2	8'	1 x 6 #2 pine	window jambs
2	10'	1 x 8 T&G pine	shutters
1	8'	1 x 4 #2 pine	shutter batten

Qty.	Size	Description	Location or Use
Door			
1	12'	1 × 8 T&G #2 pine	door
2	12'	1 × 6 #2 pine	door battens and jamb
2	10'	¼" × 1⅛" lattice	insect screen
5	12'	1 × 4 #2 pine	door trim, diagonal door brace, and corner boards
3	18"	wrought-iron strap hinges	
4 lbs.	3½"	common nails	
4 lbs.	2"	spiral- or ring-shank siding nails	
1 lb.	1¼"	galvanized deck screws	
Shelf			
1	12'	1 × 12 #2 pine	shelf
1	10'	1 × 2 #2 pine	shelf front trim
1	8'	1 × 6	tool board
1	36"	1"-diameter wooden dowel	tool pegs

Base

1. Begin by building a level base. Cut two pieces of 2 × 6 lumber to a length of 9', and two more pieces of 2 × 6, each 6'9" long. Nail them together at the corners, using 3½" common nails (see **fig. 1**). Cut four 2 × 6 P.T. floor joists, each 6'9" long, and nail them inside and at right angles to the 9'-long pieces, spaced 24" on-center. Place the last floor joist 12" from the end. These measurements are made from the outside of each side of the 2 × 6 frame and to the center of each joist (see detail, **fig. 1**).

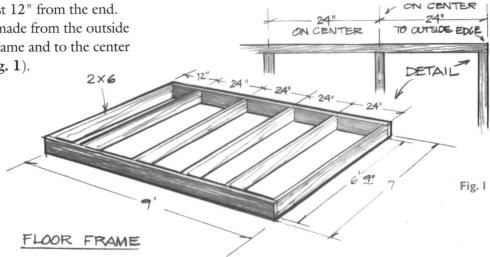

FLOOR FRAME

Fig. 1

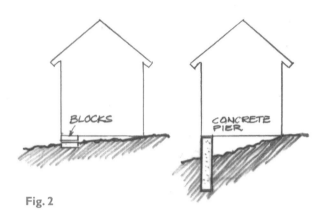

Fig. 2

2. Adjust for any unevenness in your building site by shoring up the base of the shed to make it level. Do this by laying the frame on concrete blocks at the low end of your building site. Use solid concrete half-blocks (4" × 8" × 16"), piled up on one another. Add slate shims in between the blocks and the frame to make the shed frame perfectly level. If you need more than three blocks to make the frame level, consider switching to 12"-diameter cardboard Sonatubes, buried 36" deep in the ground and filled with concrete to form piers (see **fig. 2**).

3. For several days, periodically check to make sure the frame has not settled out of level, since this could cause problems in later stages of construction.

Floor

1. Cut two pieces of ¾" exterior plywood to 4' × 7', and nail them on top of the 2 × 6 frame (see **fig. 3**). Temporarily nail all four corners of each piece of plywood to the frame, to make sure the frame is square. Use the leftover plywood to cover the 12"-wide opening at the far end of the floor.

2. Double-check for squareness by measuring the diagonals. They should measure 136⅞". Nail the plywood to the frame, using 2" siding nails at 6" intervals.

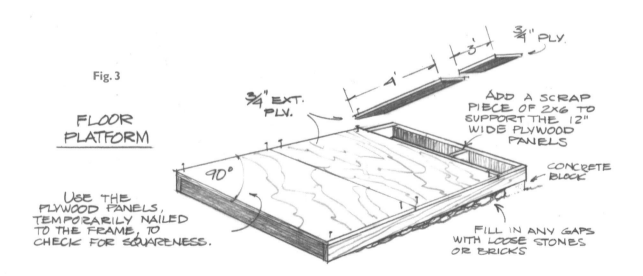

Fig. 3

FLOOR PLATFORM

USE THE PLYWOOD PANELS, TEMPORARILY NAILED TO THE FRAME, TO CHECK FOR SQUARENESS.

¾" EXT. PLY.

90°

¾" PLY.

ADD A SCRAP PIECE OF 2×6 TO SUPPORT THE 12" WIDE PLYWOOD PANELS

CONCRETE BLOCK

FILL IN ANY GAPS WITH LOOSE STONES OR BRICKS

Walls

1. Build the back wall first by cutting two 2 × 4s into 9'-long plates, and five 2 × 4s into 6'9"-long studs. Using the floor deck as a work platform, nail the 2 × 4 top and bottom plates to the ends of the studs, 26⅝" on-center, measured from the center of one stud to the center of the next (see **figs. 4 and 6**).

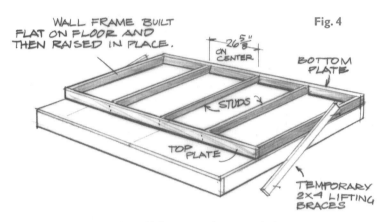

WALL FRAME BUILT FLAT ON FLOOR AND THEN RAISED IN PLACE.

Fig. 4

26 ⅝" ON CENTER

BOTTOM PLATE

STUDS

TOP PLATE

TEMPORARY 2×4 LIFTING BRACES

2. Lift up the back wall frame and secure it in place with two 2 × 4 braces nailed to the sides of the wall and to the sides of the floor frame.

3. Build the two end walls in the same way. Cut 77"-long top and bottom plates, which allows for the thickness of the front and rear walls. Cut four 6'9"-long studs for each end wall. Once they are assembled, stand them up and temporarily nail them to the back wall frame.

4. Build the front wall to the dimensions shown in the plan, doubling the number of corner studs for extra strength (see **figs. 5 and 6**). After checking to make sure all the measurements are correct and the frame is square and plumb (vertical), nail the 2 × 4s together permanently with 3½" common nails.

5. To make sure the frame stays in alignment while you are completing the structure, temporarily nail 1 × 4 diagonal braces to the inside walls. Complete the frame by cutting and nailing a second layer of 2 × 4s (cap plate) on top of the end plates (see **fig. 5**).

6. To strengthen the walls, toenail 2 × 4 nailers horizontally between the studs, 33¾" up from the floor (see **fig. 7**).

7. Cut two pieces of 2 × 4, each 25½" long, and nail them between the studs at each of the two window locations.

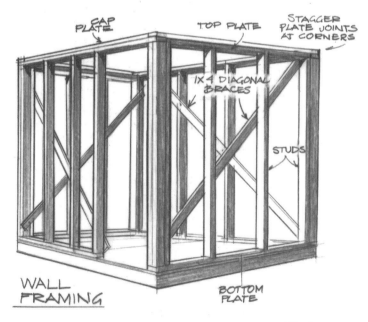

CAP PLATE

TOP PLATE

STAGGER PLATE JOINTS AT CORNERS

1X4 DIAGONAL BRACES

STUDS

WALL FRAMING

BOTTOM PLATE

Fig. 5

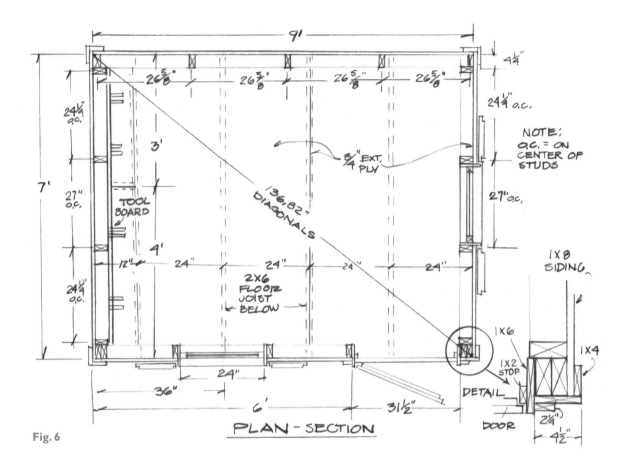

Fig. 6

PLAN – SECTION

Labels in figure: 9' • 26⅝" • 26⅝" • 26⅝" • 26⅝" • 4¼" • 24¼" o.c. • NOTE: O.C. = ON CENTER OF STUDS • 24¼" o.c. • 3' • ¾" EXT. PLY • 27" o.c. • 1X8 SIDING • 7' • 27" o.c. • TOOL BOARD • 136.82" DIAGONALS • 4' • 12" • 24" • 24" • 24" • 24" • 2X6 FLOOR JOIST BELOW • 24¼" o.c. • 1X6 • 1X2 STOP • 1X4 • DETAIL • DOOR • 2¼" • 4½" • 24" • 36" • 6' • 31½"

Fig. 7

WINDOW FRAME • 32½" • 25½" • 2X4 NAILER • 33¾"

Siding

1. To cover the walls with horizontal sheathing, you will need approximately 384 linear feet of 1 × 8 tongue-and-groove (T&G) #2 pine. Partially hammer three nails into the 2 × 6 base of each side, 1" below the ¾" plywood floor. Use them as a ledge on which to rest the bottom of the first piece of 1 × 8 sheathing (see **fig. 8**). Start at the back and work around to the front, nailing on one course at a time, using 2" spiral- or ring-shank siding nails.

2. Face nail the first row of boards at the bottom, and toenail them at the top. The remaining boards are held at the bottom by the tongue and groove, and toenailed into the tongue at the top of each successive board (see **fig. 8**). Continue until you reach the top of the plate, cutting the last course so that the board fits below the overhanging rafter.

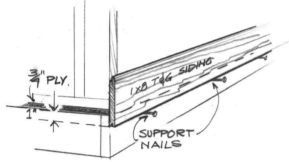

Fig. 8

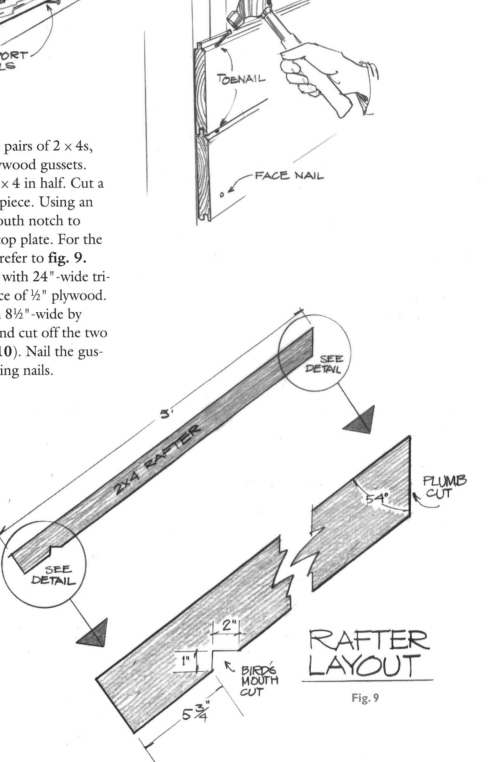

Rafters

1. The rafters consist of five pairs of 2 × 4s, joined at their peaks by ½" plywood gussets. Begin by cutting a 10'-long 2 × 4 in half. Cut a 54° angle on one end of each piece. Using an electric jig saw, cut a bird's mouth notch to allow the rafters to sit on the top plate. For the location of this bird's mouth, refer to **fig. 9.**

2. Join the rafters at the top with 24"-wide triangular gussets, cut from a piece of ½" plywood. Make the gussets by cutting an 8½"-wide by 24"-long plywood rectangle, and cut off the two sides at 36½° angles (see **fig. 10**). Nail the gussets to the rafters, using 2" siding nails.

RAFTER LAYOUT

Fig. 9

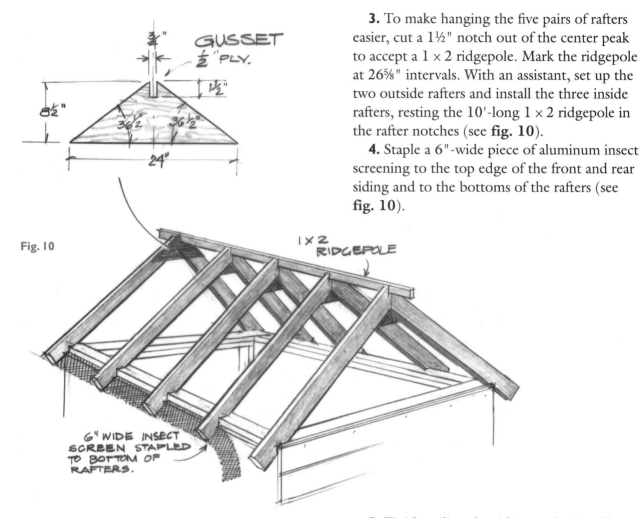

GUSSET ½" PLY.

¾"

1½"

8½"

36½° 36½°

24"

Fig. 10

1 X 2 RIDGEPOLE

6" WIDE INSECT SCREEN STAPLED TO BOTTOM OF RAFTERS.

3. To make hanging the five pairs of rafters easier, cut a 1½" notch out of the center peak to accept a 1 × 2 ridgepole. Mark the ridgepole at 26⅝" intervals. With an assistant, set up the two outside rafters and install the three inside rafters, resting the 10'-long 1 × 2 ridgepole in the rafter notches (see **fig. 10**).

4. Staple a 6"-wide piece of aluminum insect screening to the top edge of the front and rear siding and to the bottoms of the rafters (see **fig. 10**).

5. Finish nailing the siding on both gable ends of the building. Let the ends of the siding overhang the tops of the rafters, then snap a chalk line and cut them off in one pass, using an electric circular saw. Do not allow any of the siding boards to stick up above the tops of the rafters, as this will create a bump in the roof.

Finishing the Roof

1. Nail two 10'-long pieces of 1 × 4 fascia to the ends of the rafters, allowing 6" to extend beyond each end of the gable-end wall. Nail a 10'-long 1 × 6 over the rafters and the fascia (see **fig. 11**). Cut four 1 × 4s, each 5' long, for the gable trim. Cut off one end of each 1 × 4 at a 54° angle, so that they fit together neatly at the top. Notch out the tops of the 1 × 4 gable trim to accept the end of the 1 × 2 ridgepole (see **figs. 11 and 12**).

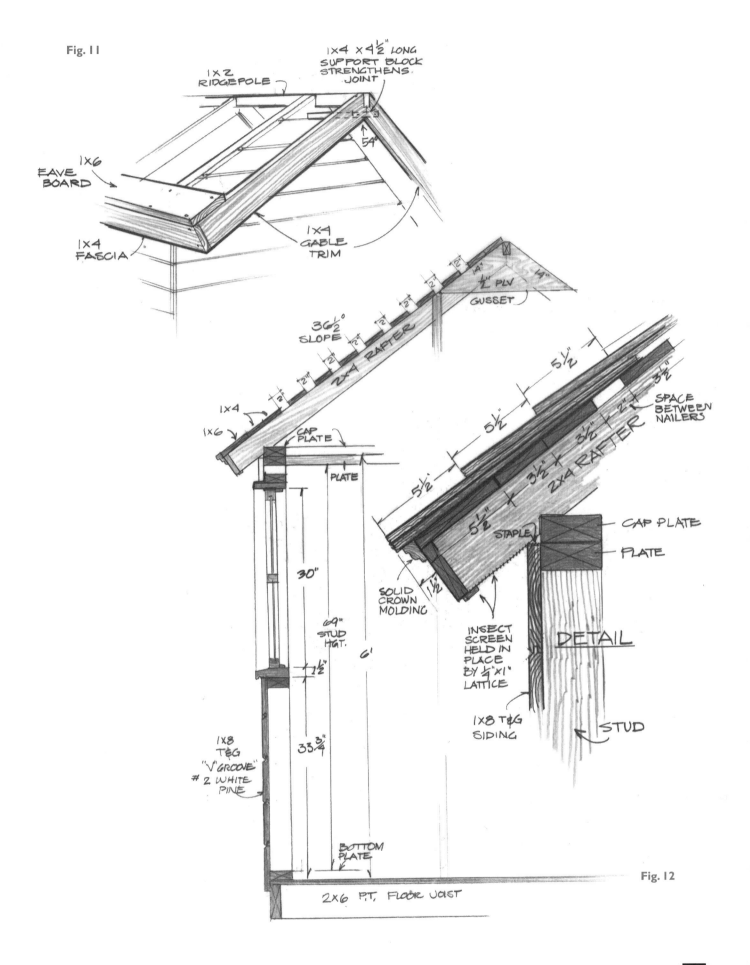

Fig. 11

1×2 RIDGEPOLE

1×4 ×4½" LONG SUPPORT BLOCK STRENGTHENS JOINT

54°

EAVE BOARD

1×6

1×4 FASCIA

1×4 GABLE TRIM

½" PLY GUSSET

1¼"

2"

36½" SLOPE

2×4 RAFTER

1×4

1×6

CAP PLATE

PLATE

5½"

5½"

3½"

3½"

2"

SPACE BETWEEN NAILERS

2×4 RAFTER

5½"

5½"

5½"

STAPLE

CAP PLATE

PLATE

DETAIL

30"

69" STUD HGT.

6'

1½"

SOLID CROWN MOLDING

1½"

INSECT SCREEN HELD IN PLACE BY ¼"×1" LATTICE

1×8 T&G SIDING

STUD

1×8 T&G "V"GROOVE # 2 WHITE PINE

33¾"

BOTTOM PLATE

2×6 P.T. FLOOR JOIST

Fig. 12

Fig. 13

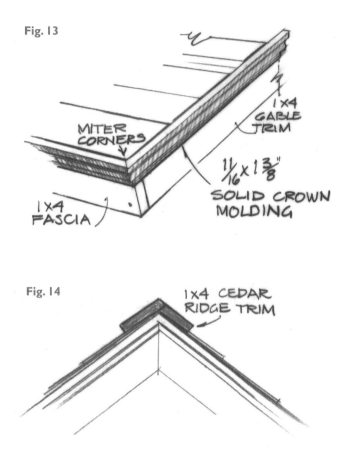

MITER
CORNERS

1×4
GABLE
TRIM

1×4
FASCIA

$\frac{11}{16}" \times 1\frac{3}{8}"$
SOLID CROWN
MOLDING

Fig. 14

1×4 CEDAR
RIDGE TRIM

2. To support the cedar shingles, nail two 10'-long 1 × 4s above each of the 1 × 6s along the eaves, using 2" siding nails. Allow a 2" space and add another nailer, continuing up the roof until you reach the peak (see **fig. 12**). Nail the ends of the nailers to the 1 × 4 gable trim.

3. Finish off the roof framing by adding $\frac{11}{16}" \times 1\frac{3}{8}"$ solid crown molding to the eaves and the gables. For a professional, finished appearance, miter the corner moldings where they meet (see **fig. 13**).

4. Use five bundles of red-cedar shingles to cover the roof. Double the first course and overlap the gables and eave edge by ½" (see detail, **fig. 12**). Nail on each course 5½" above the preceding one, making sure to stagger the shingles so the joints don't line up. Use a chalk line or straight piece of 1 × 4 to keep the lines straight. Cover the peak with two 121"-long pieces of cedar. Rip cut each at a 54° bevel along one edge before they are nailed together (see **fig. 14**).

Windows and Door

1. See Hexagonal Garden House on page 98 for instructions on building the windows. Adjust the dimensions for a 24"-wide by 30"-high sash.

2. Frame the door opening in 1 × 6 #2 pine and add a piece of 1 × 2 to the front edge of the floor at the door opening (see **fig. 15**). See Garden Shower on page 114 for instructions on building the shed door. This door will be slightly larger, measuring 30" wide by 67" high. Install three wrought-iron strap hinges to support it.

Fig. 15

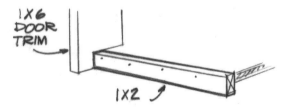

1×6
DOOR
TRIM

1×2

Finishing Touches

1. The shutters on this shed can be decorative or functional. Whether they are left natural, stained, or painted, they give the shed a more finished appearance.

2. To build shutters for two windows, cut eight pieces of 1 × 8 T&G, each 24" long. Cut 1" off the grooves of four pieces and 1" off the tongues of the other four pieces, so that the total combined width of each shutter panel measures 12". To make the horizontal battens, cut eight pieces of 1 × 4, each 10" long, and position one 3" from the bottom and one 3" from the top of each shutter (see **fig. 16**). Screw the battens to the shutters with 1¼" galvanized deck screws. For a more professional job, countersink and fill the holes with wooden plugs. Hinge or screw the shutters to both sides of each window.

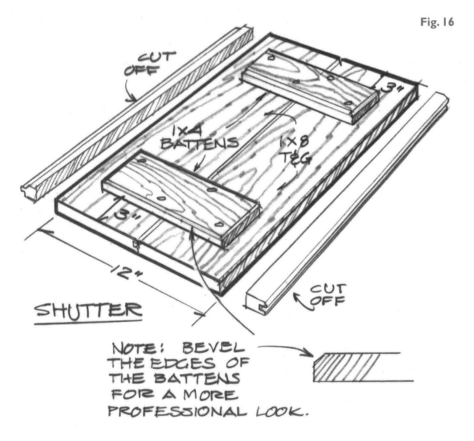

Fig. 16

CUT OFF

1×4 BATTENS

1×8 T&G

3"

3"

12"

CUT OFF

SHUTTER

NOTE: BEVEL THE EDGES OF THE BATTENS FOR A MORE PROFESSIONAL LOOK.

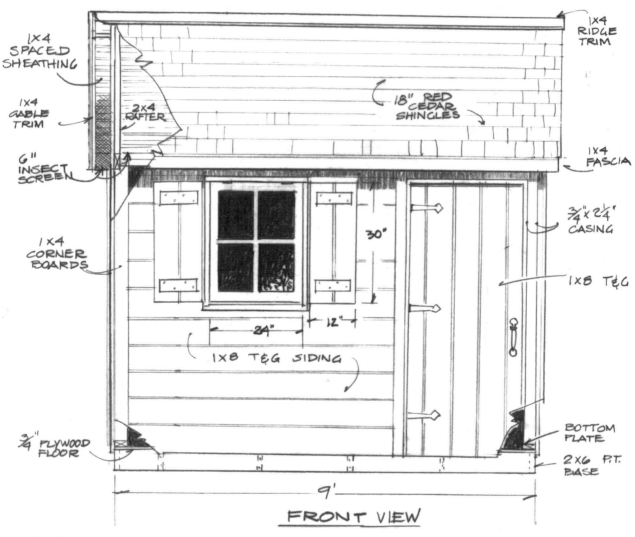

Fig. 17

Labels on figure:
- 1x4 SPACED SHEATHING
- 1x4 GABLE TRIM
- 6" INSECT SCREEN
- 1x4 CORNER BOARDS
- 2x4 RAFTER
- 18" RED CEDAR SHINGLES
- 1x4 RIDGE TRIM
- 1x4 FASCIA
- ¾" x 2¼" CASING
- 1x8 T&G
- 1x8 T&G SIDING
- 30"
- 24"
- 12"
- ¾" PLYWOOD FLOOR
- BOTTOM PLATE
- 2x6 P.T. BASE
- 9'

FRONT VIEW

3. To conceal the ends of the siding boards, add vertical 1 × 4 corner boards to the building's corners (see **fig. 17**). Notice that the corner to the right of the doorway requires a 1 × 6, ripped to 4½" and nailed to the corner studs (see **fig. 6**).

4. The door is trimmed with ¾" × 2¼" casing, ripped from a 1 × 4. Nail the trim next to both sides and to the top of the doorway.

5. As a finishing touch, nail up a 10'-long piece of ¼" × 1⅛" lattice to secure the insect screen to the bottom of the fascia (see detail, **fig. 12**). Add insect screen to the gable soffits, if desired, by stapling 6"-wide screening to the underside of the 1 × 4 spaced roof sheathing (see **fig. 17**).

6. To make a shelf, cut a 10'-long 1 × 12, so that it lies on top of the 2 × 4 horizontal nailers inside the building. Using an electric jig saw, cut out notches to accept the 2 × 4 studs. Support the shelf further by cutting a 1 × 12 diagonally to form a right triangle, and nailing it to a stud under the shelf. Attach a 1 × 2 to the front of the shelf to give it more rigidity (see **fig. 18**).

7. Build a tool board in the structure by cutting a 1 × 6 to a length of 77" and nailing it to the end wall studs. Bore ½"-diameter holes in the board, and glue 6"-long, ½"-diameter wooden dowels in the holes. The dowels are strong enough to hold most garden tools.

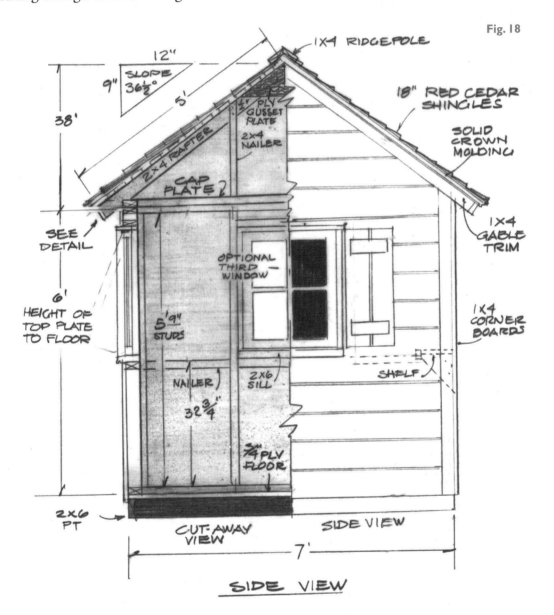

Fig. 18

Hexagonal Garden House

This classic garden shed was originally built by David's parents for his mother's garden in Summit, New Jersey, in 1937. Elegant and well suited for a formal garden, it was inspired by a colonial garden shed built for George Washington's home in Mount Vernon, Virginia. David recreated the structure in the yard behind a brownstone in New York. Six feet wide, it is large enough to store all the essential tools for your garden and still leave plenty of room for kids to disappear in when playing hide-and-seek.

Qty.	Size	Description	Location or Use
3	12'	2 x 6 P.T. lumber	base and floor joists
1	2'	2 x 6 P.T. lumber	windowsill
2	4' x 8' sheet	¾" exterior plywood	floor deck
6	8" x 8" x 8"	concrete half blocks	base
2 or 3	assorted	gray slate	shims
3	12'	4 x 4 cedar posts	corners
4	10'	2 x 4 #2 fir	plates
2	8'	2 x 2 clear cedar	window sash
1	6'	1 x 6 cedar	window jamb
2	10'	2 x 4 nailers (cats)	wall framing
22	12'	1 x 6 T&G #2 cedar	siding and door
4	12'	1 x 2 cedar	dentils and bevel support strip
2	12'	4½" sprung crown	cornice molding
2	10'	1 x 6 #2 pine	crown support
1	10'	2 x 4 #2 construction fir	temporary post
3	10'	2 x 6 #2 construction fir	rafters
3	4' x 8' sheet	½" exterior plywood	roof
1 roll	36"	15-lb. tar paper	roof
3 bundle	36"	three-tab asphalt shingles	roof
1	12'	1 x 2 #2 cedar	doorstops
1	12'	⅝ x 6 P.T. lumber	door cross braces and head jamb
1	12'	⅝ x 4 #2 pine	door casing

Hardware

Qty.	Size	Description	Location or Use
1 lb.	1½"	galvanized deck screws	door
1 lb.	3½"	galvanized deck screws	
1 lb.	2"	galvanized finishing nails	
3 lbs.	2"	spiral- or ring-shank siding nails	
2	2"	galvanized hinges	
1 dozen	1½"	copper nails	
2	18"	wrought-iron strap hinges	
1 sheet	24" x 24"	16-oz. copper sheet	
1 piece	9½" x 21½"	window glass	
1 bottle	8 oz.	waterproof yellow glue	
1		thumb latch and handle	

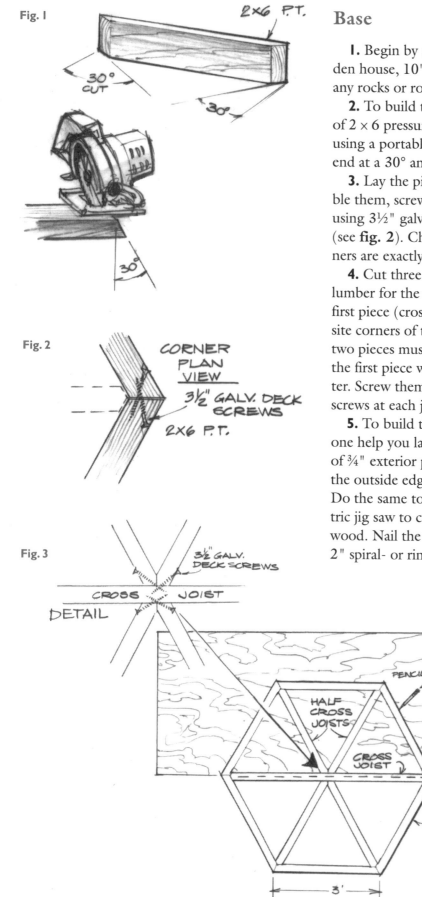

Fig. 1

2×6 P.T.

30° CUT

30°

30°

Fig. 2

CORNER
PLAN
VIEW

3½" GALV. DECK
SCREWS

2×6 P.T.

Fig. 3

3½" GALV.
DECK SCREWS

CROSS JOIST

DETAIL

HALF CROSS JOISTS

CROSS JOIST

PENCIL

¾" EXT. PLY.

P.T. BASE

3'

Base

1. Begin by making a level site for the garden house, 10' in diameter. Clear the area of any rocks or roots.

2. To build the base, cut six 36"-long pieces of 2 × 6 pressure-treated (P.T.) lumber and, using a portable circular saw, bevel cut each end at a 30° angle (see **fig.1**).

3. Lay the pieces on a flat surface and assemble them, screwing the six corners together using 3½" galvanized deck screws at each joint (see **fig. 2**). Check to make sure opposite corners are exactly 6' apart.

4. Cut three 6'-long pieces out of 2 × 6 P.T. lumber for the floor joists. Cut the ends of the first piece (cross joist) to fit into any two opposite corners of the base (see **fig. 3**). The next two pieces must be cut in half and shaped to fit the first piece where they intersect at the center. Screw them in place using four 3½" deck screws at each joint (see detail, **fig. 3**).

5. To build the plywood floor, have someone help you lay the floor frame over the sheet of ¾" exterior plywood, tracing the shape of the outside edge onto the plywood (see **fig. 3**). Do the same to the other side, and use an electric jig saw to cut out the two pieces of plywood. Nail the plywood to the base, using 2" spiral- or ring-shank nails.

6. With an assistant, move the floor base to where you want the garden house to be, and lay it on the prepared ground. If the ground is not completely level (and it rarely is), bury a concrete block at the high side under the nearest corner and prop the low side up until the base is level. Place blocks under each corner until the base is level in all directions and is solidly supported at each corner. It is important to make sure the base is absolutely level, since all subsequent work will depend on it.

7. During construction, it is possible that some of the blocks may compress into the soil, so it is a good idea to check the level of the floor each day before beginning work. If the base is not level, buy a block of slate at your lumberyard (sold expressly for this purpose), and use a claw hammer to split off small thin slabs to use as shims between the blocks and the base (see **fig. 4**).

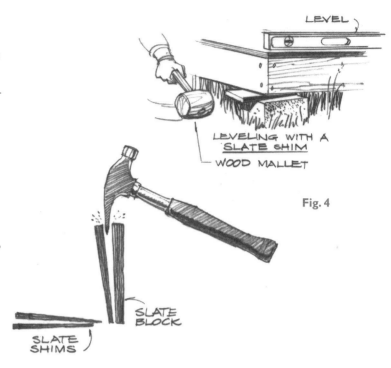

LEVEL

LEVELING WITH A SLATE SHIM

WOOD MALLET

Fig. 4

SLATE BLOCK

SLATE SHIMS

Wall Framing

I. This garden house uses one 4 × 4 post at each of the six corners. To provide a good nailing surface for the siding, two edges of each post must be ripped at 30° angles (see **fig. 5**). Cut each post 68½" long and either toenail them or screw them to the base. Connect the tops of the posts with 2 × 4 top plates laid flat. Cut each 2 × 4 top plate 36" long, and miter cut each end at a 60° angle (see **fig. 6**). Screw them to the tops of the six posts. Check frequently to make sure the structure is positioned correctly by measuring the diagonals and checking for plumb and square, using a level and a framing square.

2. Add a second layer of 2 × 4s (called cap plates) over the top wall plate, so it is offset by ¾" and protrudes out the same thickness as the siding you will install (see **fig. 6**). This will allow the cap plate to cover the top of the siding and act as a solid base for the dentils. These pieces should also be cut at a 60° miter, but will be longer (approximately 38" along the outside edge) than the top plates because they protrude further.

Fig. 5

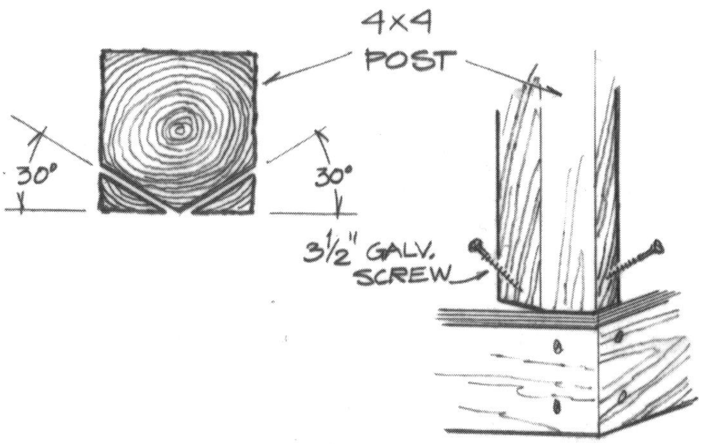

4×4 POST

30°   30°

3½" GALV. SCREW

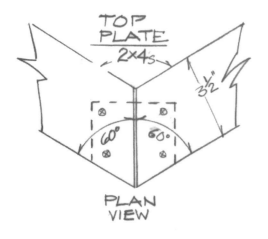

Fig. 6

TOP PLATE 2×4s

60° 60°

½"
3½"

PLAN VIEW

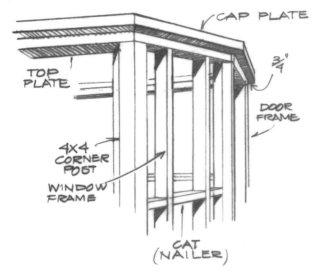

CAP PLATE

TOP PLATE

DOOR FRAME

¾"

4X4 CORNER POST

WINDOW FRAME

CAT (NAILER)

3. Frame the window and the door using 2 × 4s. Measure and cut the studs to fit perfectly between the bottom of the top plate and the plywood floor.

4. Cut 2 × 4 nailers (sometimes called cats) approximately 34½" long, so they fit between each vertical stud and each corner post (see **fig. 6**). Screw them to the studs and posts, 36" up from the floor.

Window

Since the window can be built independently from the garden house, it is a good project to tackle on a rainy day. You may think that a 1'-wide window is a waste of time, since it provides only a little light to the interior; however, this is exactly the kind of extravagance that lends quality to this design and contributes to the elegance of the structure.

The window can be made very inexpensively and quickly if you have access to a table saw; otherwise, you will have to order a window custom-made from your lumberyard. The reason this window is so easy to make is because it uses only one piece of glass instead of several small window panes. The muntin bars are applied to both sides of the glass or plastic to give the impression of truly divided lights.

I. Since there is so little wood required, select only the best available clear stock. Buy 2 × 2 clear cedar from your lumberyard, and use it to make both the window sash and the muntin bars.

Fig. 7

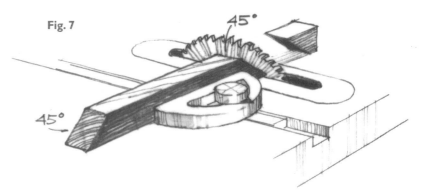

45°

45°

2. Using a table saw, cut out the four pieces for the window sash from the 2 × 2 clear cedar. The two long sides (stiles) measure 24" long. The two short sides (rails) measure 12" long. Cut 45° bevels on each end (see **fig. 7**).

3. Locate the center points where the muntin bars will join the frame, and cut ⅝" × ⅜" dadoes (see **fig. 8**).

Fig. 8

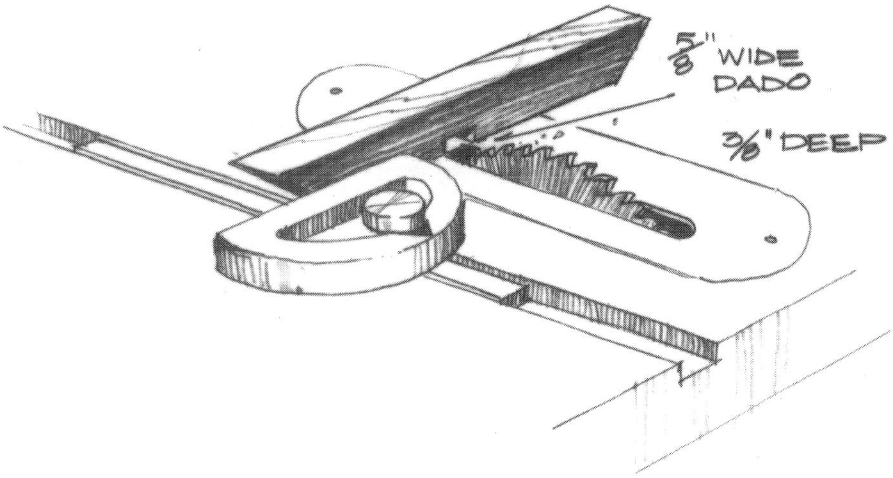

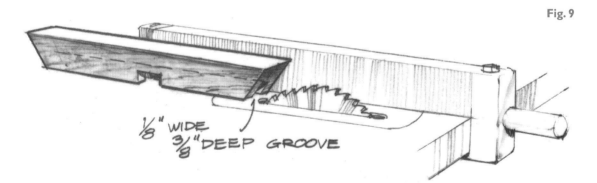

4. To hold the window glass, make a ⅛"-wide by ⅜"-deep groove in the center of the inside face of each piece of the window sash (see **fig. 9**). Cut a piece of ⅛"-thick glass to fit into the groove. To cut the glass, score the surface several times with an inexpensive glass cutter, then place the scored line along a sharp edge and snap it apart.

Fig. 9

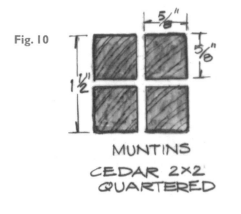

Fig. 10

MUNTINS
CEDAR 2×2
QUARTERED

5. To make the muntin bars, cut a piece of 2 × 2 in half lengthwise with a table saw. Place one of the two pieces cut-side down on the table saw, and make another cut lengthwise again; repeat with the second piece so that you have four identical ⅝"-square pieces (see **fig. 10**). Test to make sure that they fit perfectly into the dadoes.

6. To join the window stiles and rails together at the four corners, cut a 2" slot in the end of each 2 × 2 (see **fig. 11**). Make sure each slot is exactly in the center of the wood. Cut four 2" × 2" right triangles out of a scrap piece of ⅛" plywood; they should be the width of your saw blade. Trial fit them into the corners (see **fig. 11**).

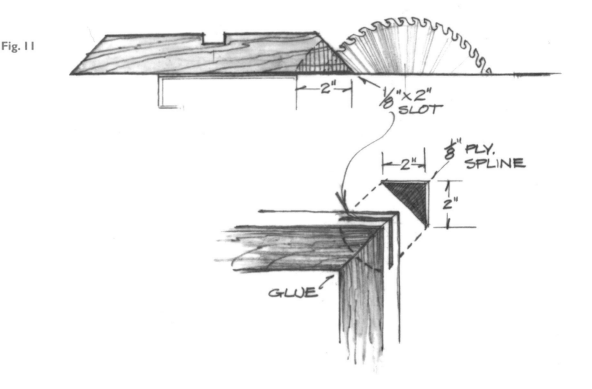

Fig. 11

⅛"×2"
SLOT

2"

⅛" PLY.
SPLINE

2"

2"

GLUE

7. Temporarily assemble the window sash, including the scrap plywood triangles. Measure and cut the muntin bars to fit in the ⅝" × ⅜" grooves in the window sash. Mark and notch out where the muntin bars intersect. After checking that all the pieces fit perfectly, squeeze a bead of silicone into the grooves in the window sash and set the piece of glass into the bed of silicone. Glue all the joints together using

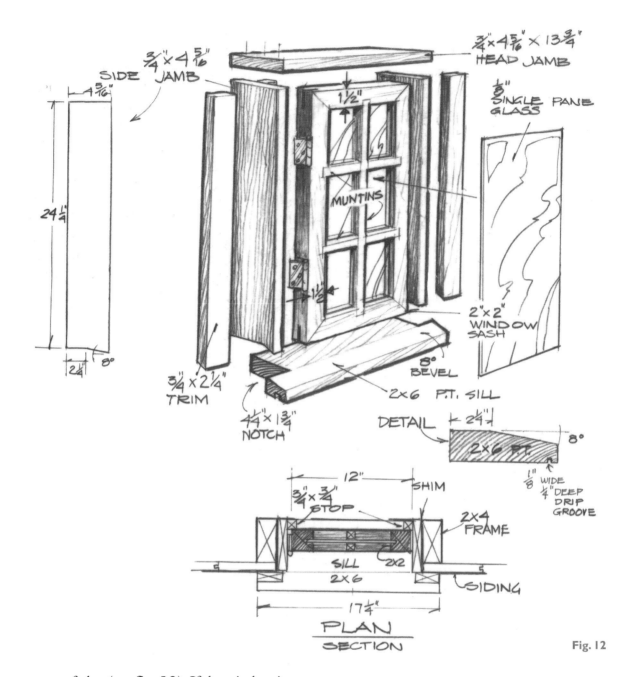

SIDE JAMB $\frac{3}{4}$" × 4 $\frac{5}{16}$"

4 $\frac{5}{16}$"

24 $\frac{1}{4}$"

2 $\frac{1}{4}$"   8°

$\frac{3}{4}$" × 4 $\frac{5}{16}$" × 13 $\frac{3}{4}$"
HEAD JAMB

$\frac{1}{8}$"
SINGLE PANE
GLASS

1 $\frac{1}{2}$"

MUNTINS

1 $\frac{1}{2}$"

2" × 2"
WINDOW
SASH

$\frac{3}{4}$" × 2 $\frac{1}{4}$"
TRIM

4 $\frac{1}{4}$" × 1 $\frac{3}{4}$"
NOTCH

8°
BEVEL

2×6 P.T. SILL

DETAIL

2 $\frac{1}{4}$"

2×6 P.T.

8°

$\frac{1}{8}$" WIDE
$\frac{1}{4}$" DEEP
DRIP
GROOVE

12"

SHIM

$\frac{3}{4}$" × $\frac{3}{4}$"
STOP

2×4
FRAME

2×2

SILL
2×6

SIDING

17 $\frac{1}{4}$"

PLAN
SECTION

Fig. 12

waterproof glue (see **fig. 12**). If the window is going to be painted, you can achieve a more professional appearance by painting the muntin bars before installing them over the glass.

8. To make the finished window frame, begin by cutting a scrap piece of 2 × 6 to a length of 17¼". Cut a 1¾" × 4¼" notch, leaving 1¼"-wide "ears" on the outside of the window-sill, then rip an 8° bevel along the top outside edge, and cut a ¼"-deep kerf (groove) along the bottom outside to create a drip line (see **fig. 12**).

9. Rip the 1 × 6 cedar to 4⁵⁄₁₆" wide, then cut two jambs to length, as shown in the side jamb detail of **fig. 12.** Cut the head jamb 13¾" long, and nail the jambs together, using 2½" galvanized finish nails. Install the 2" galvanized hinges on the window sash and hang the sash in the finished jamb. Using the offcuts left over from ripping the jamb, cut window stops to length (about 24¼"), and nail them along the inside of the sash (see **fig. 12**).

Siding

1. This garden house can be sheathed in rough 1 × 6 tongue-and-groove (T&G) cedar or, if you plan on painting it, smooth T&G cedar or pine. You will need approximately 37 pieces, each 6' long, to cover the entire structure (see **fig. 13**).

2. Starting at the right hand side of the door, cut 1" off the groove side of one of the boards, so that the edge of the board is square, and face nail it along the door frame, using 2" spiral- or ring-shank nails every 6". Nail a 2 × 4 so that it is parallel to and level with the base, to act as a temporary ledge on which to rest the boards (see **fig. 13**). Slide each succeeding board onto the groove of the preceding one and pound it in place, using a scrap piece of T&G to protect the edge.

3. The boards are toenailed to the top plate, the bottom frame, and the 2 × 4 nailer, using 2" siding nails. By toenailing the T&G boards through the tongue, you will avoid having any nails show (see detail, **fig. 13**). There is no need to nail the left side of the board, since it is held by the tongue and groove. When you get to a corner, mark where the board extends past the post. Set your saw to 30°, and rip two boards. Join the boards so that they fit neatly together at the corner. Continue around the garden house until you reach the other side of the door. Cut off the last board (to the left of the door) at right angles.

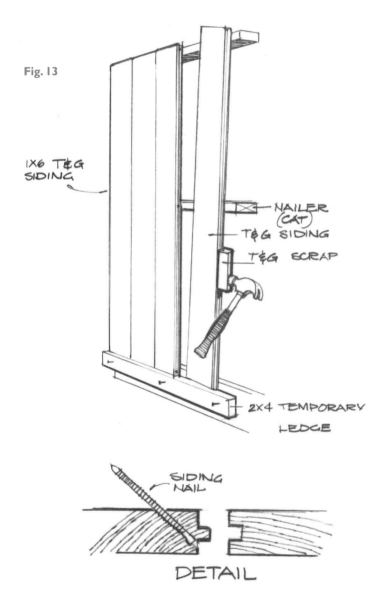

Fig. 13

1X6 T&G SIDING

NAILER (CAT)

T&G SIDING

T&G SCRAP

2X4 TEMPORARY LEDGE

SIDING NAIL

DETAIL

Dentils

From a clear piece of 1 × 2 cedar, cut 72 pieces to a length of 1¾", and 72 pieces to a length of 3½". Glue and nail them vertically to the front face of the cap plate, overlapping the top of the siding, so that they alternate in size: long, short, long, short (see **fig. 14**).

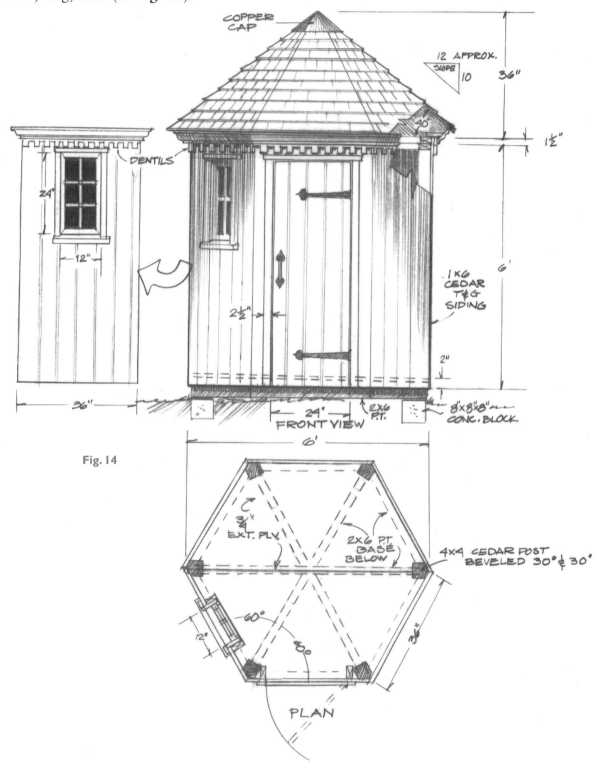

Fig. 14

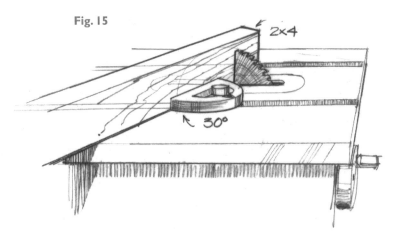

Fig. 15

Cornice

1. To make the cornice, cut six pieces of 4½"-wide sprung crown molding into 48" lengths. This dimension allows you a few extra inches at each end for adjustments. Using scrap lumber, make a miter jig to hold the molding while you are making your cuts. Since the roof is six-sided, both ends of each strip of the cornice have to be cut off at a compound angle. To facilitate these cuts, build a simple jig with the correct angle cut in the jig to use as a cutting guide.

2. To construct the jig, use two 40"-long scrap pieces of lumber, one 2 × 6 and the other 2 × 4. Measure 6" from each end of the 2 × 4 toward the center, and make a 30° cut, sawing into the wood as far as the blade will allow (see **fig. 15**). Screw the two pieces of wood together at right angles. Nail a 40"-long strip of ¾" × ¾" wood to the 2 × 6 to hold the molding in place when cutting through it (see **fig. 16**).

3. Before cutting the crown molding, measure the distance between each of the adjacent top corners of the shed. Turn the crown molding upside down in the jig, and place a hand saw in the guide cut of the jig to make a 30° compound cut at the end of each piece of cornice (see **fig. 16**).

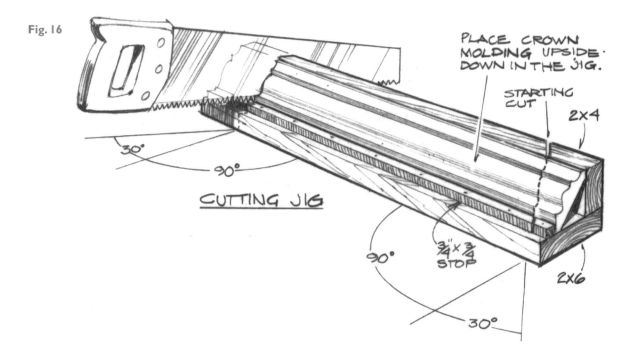

Fig. 16

4. Crown molding is sprung at a 45° angle (see **fig. 17**), but in some areas of the country, only 38° sprung molding is available. Temporarily nail the crown molding onto a beveled (in our case, 45°) 36"-long 1 × 6 (crown support), and rest it on the cap plate to test it for fit. If the crown molding doesn't fit perfectly, make slight adjustments by shaving the ends with a belt sander. Make a ¹³⁄₁₆" × ¹³⁄₁₆" triangular support strip to fit in between the crown molding and the 1 × 6 (crown support): Cut a piece of scrap lumber at a 45° bevel, and glue it to the back of the crown molding and the bottom front edge of the 1 × 6 (see **fig. 17**). When all the pieces of molding fit together perfectly, glue and screw the 1 × 6 crown support to the cap plate and to the outside of the dentils.

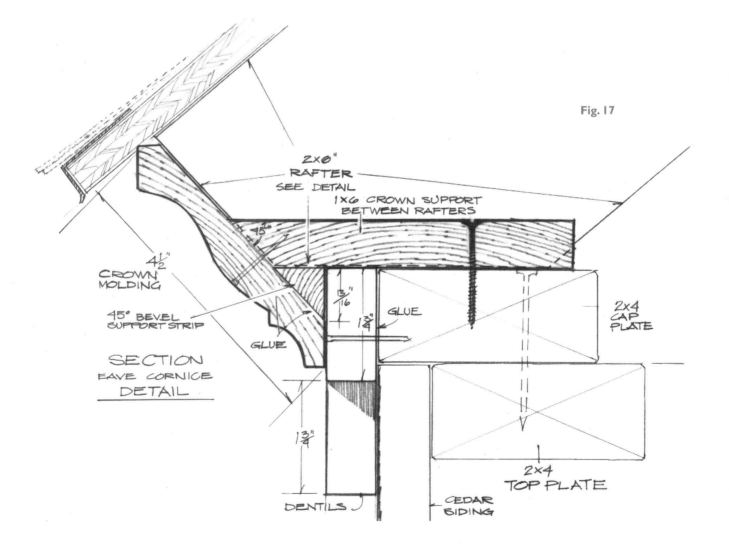

Fig. 17

2x0" RAFTER
SEE DETAIL

1x6 CROWN SUPPORT
BETWEEN RAFTERS

45°

4½"
CROWN MOLDING

45° BEVEL SUPPORT STRIP

GLUE

¹³⁄₁₆"

1¾"

GLUE

2x4 CAP PLATE

SECTION EAVE CORNICE DETAIL

1¾"

2x4 TOP PLATE

DENTILS

CEDAR SIDING

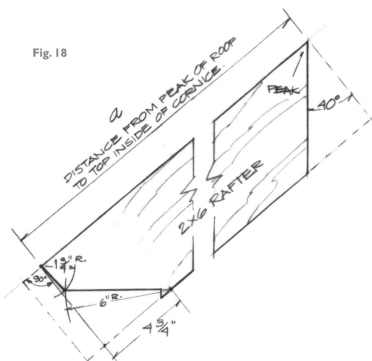

Fig. 18

a DISTANCE FROM PEAK OF ROOF TO TOP INSIDE OF CORNICE.

PEAK

40°

2×6 RAFTER

1¾" R.

90°

6" R.

4⅝"

Rafters

1. Cut one end of a 5'-long 2 × 6 rafter at a 40° angle. This will be the peak of the rafter (see **fig. 18**).

2. To determine the final length of the rafter, you must first locate a point 8'10" up from the center of the structure. Do this by temporarily toenailing a 9'-long piece of scrap 2 × 4 lumber to the exact center of the floor (see **fig. 19**). Hold it in place by nailing a cross brace to the cap plates. Measure up from the floor 8'10" on the temporary center post, and drive in a nail at this point. Measure from this point diagonally down to the top inside edge of the cornice. Using this dimension, measure from the peak of the rafter down to the opposite end and make a mark. Cut off the bottom end of one rafter as shown in **fig. 18**. Do the same for the rafter that will be placed opposite this one.

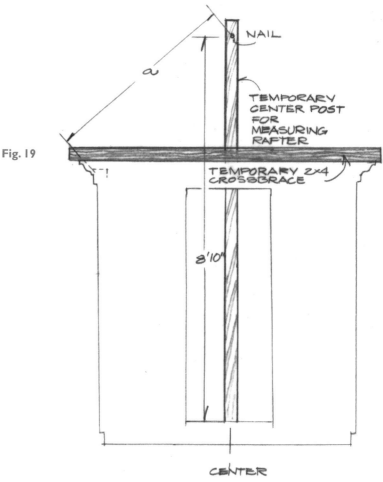

Fig. 19

NAIL

a

TEMPORARY CENTER POST FOR MEASURING RAFTER

TEMPORARY 2×4 CROSSBRACE

8'10"

CENTER

3. Raise the first pair of rafters, temporarily nailing them together at the peak. Use the center pole to hold them in place. The next two pairs of rafters join the first pair at the peak (see **fig. 20**). These will be slightly shorter than the first pair and will have two beveled cuts on the end at the peak in order for them to fit together neatly. Remove the temporary center post and screw them together, using 3½" galvanized deck screws.

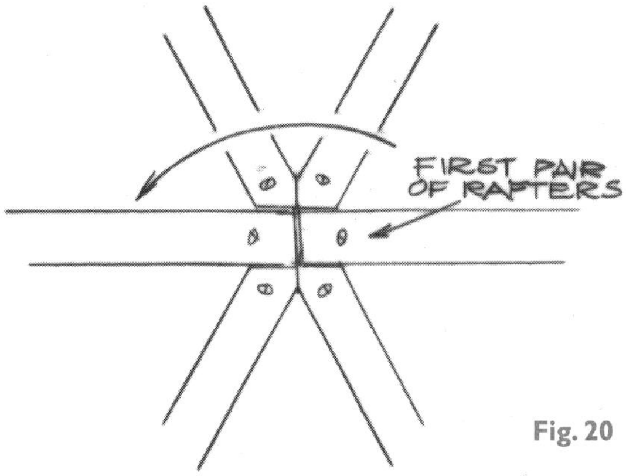

Roof

The roof is sheathed with ½" exterior plywood. Each triangular piece will be approximately 4'10" along a long edge, allowing for a 1" overhang at the eaves (see **fig. 21**). Check and adjust these dimensions to match your conditions. You will be able to cut two roof panels out of a single 4 × 8 piece of plywood. Use a chalk line to mark the cut lines. Set your saw blade at 10° and cut out the pieces. Nail the wedge-shaped panels to the rafters using 2" nails, and cover the roof with 15-pound tar paper and asphalt shingles.

FIRST PAIR OF RAFTERS

Fig. 20

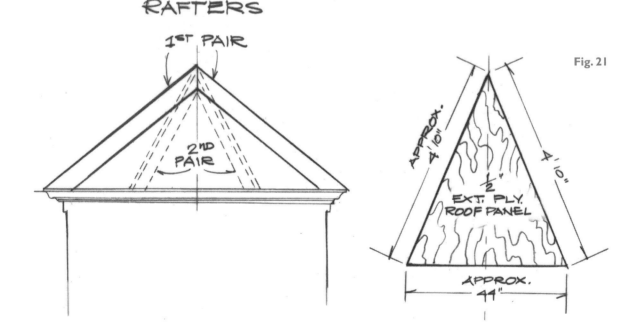

RAFTERS

1ST PAIR

2ND PAIR

Fig. 21

APPROX. 4'10"

4'10"

½" EXT. PLY. ROOF PANEL

APPROX. 44"

Door

1. Begin building the door by making a 29"-long head jamb out of $\frac{5}{4} \times 6$ P.T. lumber. Cut a notch out of each end so that the head jamb will fit inside the door opening, yet extend $\frac{1}{4}$" past the $2\frac{1}{4}$"-wide door trim on each side. Install this head jamb under the 2×4 top plate, using $2\frac{1}{2}$" finishing nails (see **fig. 22**).

2. To establish the height of the door, measure the distance from under the head jamb to the bottom of the siding. Cut five pieces of 1×6 T&G cedar to this dimension. Lay the pieces on two sawhorses, backside up, and join them together. Rip the two outside boards of the door, so that the door measures $23\frac{3}{4}$", allowing clearance for the door to open and close (see front view, **fig. 14**). Cut two $\frac{5}{4}$" $\times 6$ P.T. crosspieces, each $21\frac{1}{2}$" long, and screw them to the back of the door, using $1\frac{1}{2}$" galvanized deck screws. For a perfect job, countersink each screw and bevel the edges of the two battens.

Fig. 22

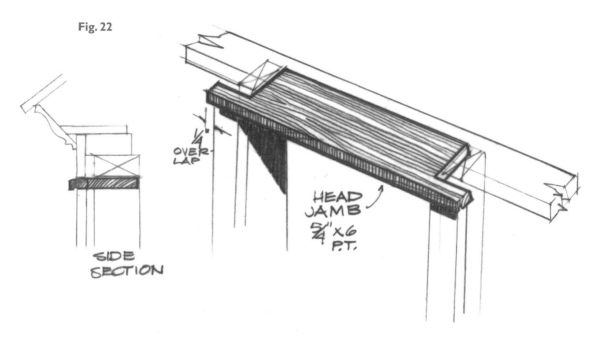

OVERLAP $\frac{1}{4}$"

HEAD JAMB $\frac{5}{4}$" x 6 P.T.

SIDE SECTION

3. Strengthen the door by running a $\frac{5}{4} \times 4$ diagonal brace from the top side opposite the hinges down to the lower hinge side (see Garden Shower on page 114). Hang the door from two 18" black strap hinges.

4. To provide a surface for the door to rest against when it swings shut, cut two pieces of 1×2, 6' long, to act as a doorstop. Cut them to fit the sides of the door. Stand inside the garden house with the door closed and nail them in place, using $2\frac{1}{2}$" galvanized finishing nails.

Cap

To top off this elegant garden structure, it's easy to make a copper cap that fits over the peak of the roof and keeps out the rain. Find the center of a 24"-square sheet of 16-ounce copper, and cut out a 24"-diameter circle. Mark and cut a straight line from one edge to the center (along the radius) of the piece of copper, and bend it into the shape of a rough cone, overlapping the edges. After fitting the cone to the peak of the roof, nail it on securely, using $1\frac{1}{2}$" copper nails.

To make hanging the door easier, attach the hinges to the door trim (casing) piece before attaching the trim to the house, screwing the hinges onto the door first and then onto the $2\frac{1}{4}$"-wide door trim (ripped from $\frac{5}{4} \times 4$ #2 pine). Attach a handle to the door to give you something to hold on to while you are installing it. Support the bottom of the door with the toe of your boot and, when you are sure it is aligned properly, nail the door trim onto the siding.

DOOR HEAD JAMB

DOOR ATTACHED TO $2\frac{1}{4}$" DOOR TRIM

$2\frac{1}{2}$" GALV. FINISH NAILS

Garden Shower

There's nothing like showering outside for cleaning up. Open-air showering provides a wonderful way to relax after working in the garden, and enables you to rinse off and enter the house feeling refreshed. The side of the garden shower can serve as a backdrop for brightly colored annuals or a fragrant rose bush. The plants will thrive on being regularly watered!

This garden shower was originally designed and built by our good friend Bill Biery, a television newscaster by profession and an occasional weekend carpenter. We altered the design slightly by installing tongue-and-groove boards diagonally, creating a herringbone effect, and adding an indoor shower bench. A brick walkway leads from the shower door to the deck.

Qty.	Size	Description	Location or Use
5	8'	4 × 4 cedar posts	frame posts
1	6'	2 × 4 cedar	side frame
1	10'	2 × 4 cedar	front frame
15	8'	1 × 6 clear cedar T&G, V-groove	door, front panel, and side panel
1	12'	1 × 4 #2 cedar	top trim
2	8'	1 × 6 #2 cedar	cap trim
1	14'	1 × 6 #2 cedar	front panel trim
2	10'	1 × 6 #2 cedar	door battens, braces, and trim
1	12'	5/4 × 4 cedar	seat
5	10'	5/4 × 4 redwood or cedar decking	interior floor decking and seat cleats
1	12'	2 × 4 P.T. lumber	floor joists
1	6"	thumb latch	door
1	36"	1"-diameter wooden dowel	pegboard
2	3½"	galvanized, self-closing door hinges	
1	3"	hook-and-eye	
1 lb.	2"	galvanized finishing nails	
1 lb.	1¼"	galvanized deck screws	
6	⅜ × 6"	lag screws with washers	

Frame

1. This garden shower is built on five sturdy 4 × 4 cedar posts. To protect the bottoms from dry rot and insect infestations, soak them in wood preservative and coat them with wax or roofing tar (see Posts and Gates on page 7).

2. Once you have decided where you want to build the shower enclosure, measure and mark where the first two post holes will be dug against the side of the house. They should be 5' apart and 18" deep. Measure out 3' from the first two post holes, and set two stakes 5' apart. Check to see if the stakes are square with the house by measuring the distance diagonally from corner to corner (see **fig. 1**). Both measurements should be the same (approximately 70"). Cut a third stake and place it equidistant between the two front stakes. Remove all three stakes, and in their place dig three 6"-diameter, 18"-deep holes. Cut one 78"-long 4 × 4 for

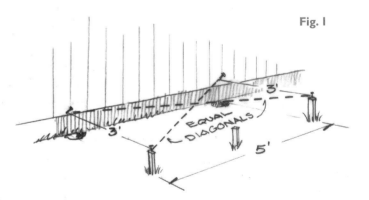

Fig. 1

Fig. 2

1×6 CAP

45° MITER

1×4 TOP TRIM

2×4s 29"

78" 4×4 CENTER POST

⅜" × 6" LAG SCREWS

4×4 POSTS

29¾" 2×4

SHOWER ENCLOSURE FRAME

the front center post, and place this in its hole. Place an 8'-long 4 × 4 in each of the other holes. Do not backfill until later.

3. To attach the first two posts to the house, drill three holes, each ½" in diameter, in both posts and screw ⅜" × 6" lag screws through the holes and into the house. Always turn off the electricity when drilling into the wall of a house, and for convenience use a battery operated drill if you have one.

4. To connect and trim out the tops of the posts, cut a 61½"-long piece of 1 × 4, and nail it to the top front of the front two corner posts. Leave a ¾" overhang at each end. Cut two more 1 × 4 boards, each 36" long, and nail them to the top sides, spanning the distance between the posts attached to the house and the front two corner posts (see **fig. 2**).

5. Cap the tops of the corner posts and the trim pieces with 1 × 6 boards laid flat and mitered 45° at the two outside corners of the shower enclosure (see **fig. 2**).

6. To frame the top of the front panel, cut a 53"-long piece of 2 × 4; toenail it between the two front corner posts, 5' up from the ground, and nail it into the top of the center post.

7. To frame the bottom of the front panel, cut two pieces of 2 × 4, each 24¾" long, and toenail them between the front corner posts and the center post, 12" up from the ground. Toenail two more 2 × 4s, each 29" long, between the two side posts opposite where the door will be (see **figs. 2 and 3**). Check that the structure is square and plumb, then backfill the holes.

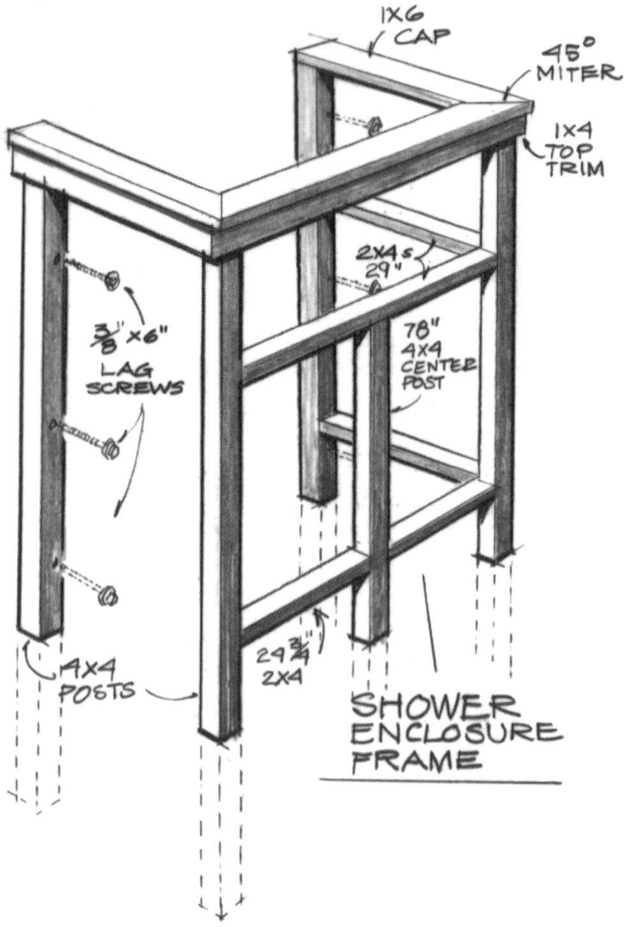

Panels and Trim

1. Cover the front of the shower enclosure with 1 × 6 T&G cedar. Cut the ends off at 45° angles, and nail them diagonally to the 4 × 4 posts and to the 2 × 4 horizontal frame (see front view, **fig. 3**).

2. Cover the right side of the shower enclosure with vertical 1 × 6 T&G boards, overlapping the front diagonal T&G boards by 1".

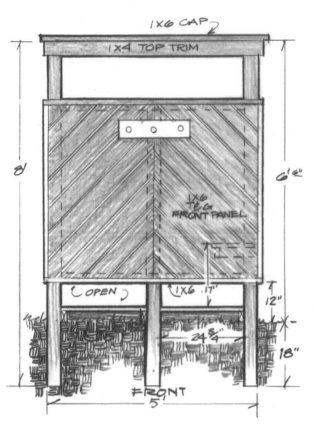

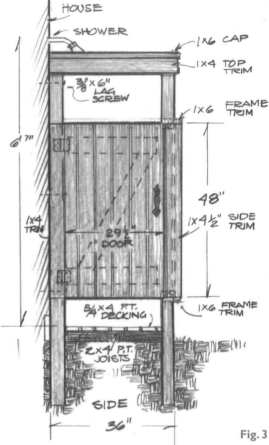

Fig. 3

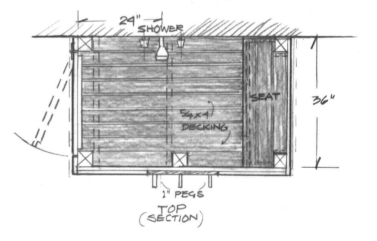

3. To trim the frame of the front panel, install a 61½"-long 1 × 6 to the top and bottom of the panel. Cut a 3½" × 3½" notch out of the two back corners of the trim so that it can fit around the two corner posts (see **fig. 4a**). Cut a 3½" × 3½" notch out of the middle of the bottom piece of 1 × 6 to accept the center 4 × 4 post.

4. In preparation for hanging the door, rip two 4'-long pieces of 1 × 6 T&G, one 3½" wide and another 4½" wide. These will be the left and right trim pieces. Nail the right trim piece in place, overlapping the front panel by 1" and making it flush with the front panel trim (see **fig. 4b**).

5. Temporarily nail the left trim piece of the door enclosure to the post that is attached to the house. The distance between the two pieces of trim should be approximately 30".

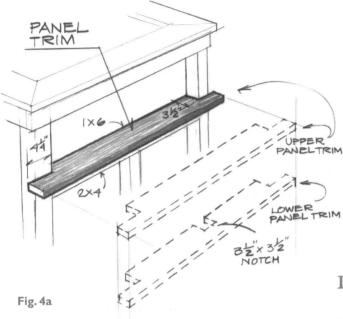

PANEL TRIM

1×6

3½"

4¼"

2×4

Fig. 4a

UPPER PANEL TRIM

LOWER PANEL TRIM

3½" × 3½" NOTCH

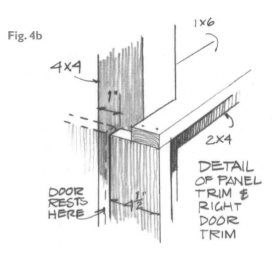

Fig. 4b

1×6

4×4

1"

2×4

DETAIL OF PANEL TRIM & RIGHT DOOR TRIM

DOOR RESTS HERE

1½"

Door and Seat

1. Fit together six 4'-long pieces of 1 × 6 T&G. Rip the left and right edges square so that the assembled six pieces measure about 29½" wide. Cut two battens from 28¼"-long 1 × 6s; screw them to the backs of the six 1 × 6 T&G, 4" from the top and bottom, flush with one edge, using 1¼" galvanized deck screws. Place another piece of 1 × 6 diagonally across the door, with the ends overlapping the two battens. Mark where the diagonal brace meets the two 1 × 6 battens, and cut off the overlapping board at these marks (see **fig. 5**). Fit the diagonal brace between the two battens and screw it to the back of the door, using 1¼" galvanized deck screws.

2. Screw two 3½" galvanized self-closing hinges, 5" from the top and bottom of the door, and screw the door to the left trim piece

Fig. 5

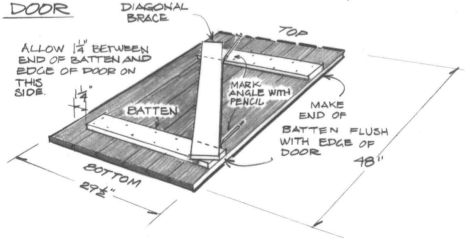

DOOR

DIAGONAL BRACE

TOP

ALLOW 1¼" BETWEEN END OF BATTEN AND EDGE OF DOOR ON THIS SIDE.

1¼"

BATTEN

MARK ANGLE WITH PENCIL

MAKE END OF BATTEN FLUSH WITH EDGE OF DOOR

BOTTOM 29½"

48"

and post. The door will rest and close on the 1"-wide exposed lip of the 4 × 4 corner post.

3. Install a thumb latch (operable from two sides) and a hook-and-eye for added security on the inside of the door.

4. Build a 36"-wide seat from ⁵⁄₄ × 4 cedar. For the seat top, cut three 36"-long pieces and one 29"-long piece (see **fig. 6**). Cut two 7"-long cleats and two 3½"-long cleats. Nail them to the house, front panel, and 4 × 4 side posts (see **fig. 3**). Nail the front of the seat to the front edge of the 7"-long cleats, and nail the top pieces to the side cleats, using 2" galvanized finishing nails.

5. Build an optional ledge for soap and shampoo out of a piece of scrap 1 × 4, toe-nailed between two of the front posts.

Floor

1. For the floor decking, cut three 36"-long pieces of 2 × 4 P.T. lumber, and nail them to the bottom of the 4 × 4 posts inside the shower stall (see side view, **fig. 3**). Check to make sure they are level in all directions. Cut seven pieces of ⁵⁄₄ × 4 redwood or cedar lumber, and screw them to the 2 × 4 joists, using 1½" galvanized deck screws. Cut a 53"-long piece of ⁵⁄₄ × 4 P.T. lumber to fit between the back posts, and two 24¾"-long pieces to fit between the front and center posts. Screw them in place.

2. As a final touch, build a pegboard from a leftover scrap of 1 × 4, measuring about 21" long. Drill a 1"-diameter hole in the center, and drill two additional holes 8" from the center peg. Cut three pieces of 1"-diameter dowel, each to a length of 4", and glue them into the holes (see **fig. 7**). Screw the pegboard to the center of the front panel, 6" from the top.

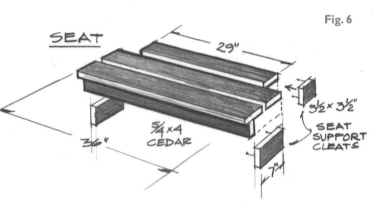

Fig. 6

SEAT

29"

3½ × 3½

SEAT SUPPORT CLEATS

36"

⁵⁄₄ × 4 CEDAR

7"

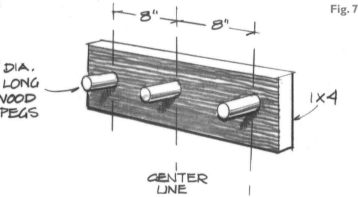

Fig. 7

8"

8"

1" DIA. 4" LONG WOOD PEGS

1 × 4

CENTER LINE

Child's Secret Garden Retreat

Choose a sunny spot in your garden for this playhouse, and build it at the end of a path, so it comes as a surprise when you encounter it. This open-air structure, made of lattice and canvas, makes a wonderful garden retreat in which your kids can practice being junior gardeners. They can get seeds started, arrange bouquets for tea parties or lemonade breaks, meet with their friends, or just use it as a quiet place to read or do their homework. Plant roses or clematis in front of the trellis walls, and weave the stems through the openings. This garden playhouse will soon look as if it is made of blossoms.

The following instructions are for a brick and timber base; however, if you want to build a temporary structure that can be easily moved, make the base out of pressure-treated lumber and use screws rather than nails.

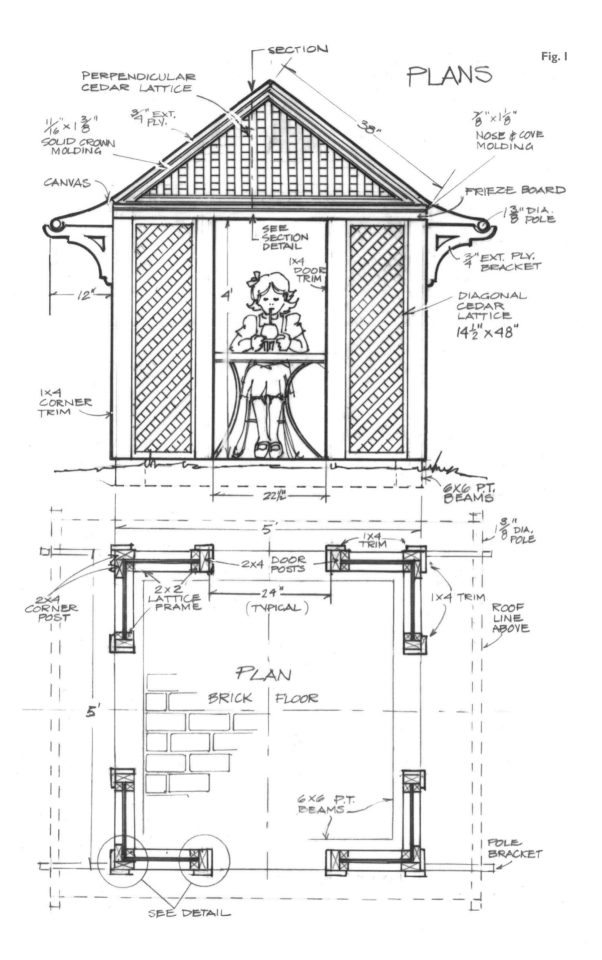

PLANS

Fig. 1

SECTION

PERPENDICULAR
CEDAR LATTICE

$\frac{11}{16}$" × $1\frac{3}{8}$"
SOLID CROWN
MOLDING

$\frac{3}{4}$" EXT.
PLY.

38"

$\frac{7}{8}$" × $1\frac{1}{8}$"
NOSE & COVE
MOLDING

CANVAS

FRIEZE BOARD

$1\frac{3}{8}$" DIA.
POLE

12"

SEE
SECTION
DETAIL

1×4
DOOR
TRIM

4'

$\frac{3}{4}$" EXT. PLY.
BRACKET

DIAGONAL
CEDAR
LATTICE
$14\frac{1}{2}$" × 48"

1×4
CORNER
TRIM

22$\frac{1}{2}$"

6×6 P.T.
BEAMS

5'

$\frac{3}{8}$" DIA.
POLE

2×4 CORNER
POST

2×2
LATTICE
FRAME

1×4
TRIM

2×4 DOOR
POSTS

24"
(TYPICAL)

1×4 TRIM

ROOF
LINE
ABOVE

5'

PLAN

BRICK   FLOOR

6×6 P.T.
BEAMS

POLE
BRACKET

SEE DETAIL

Materials Needed

Qty.	Size	Description	Location or Use
2	10'	6 x 6 P.T. lumber	base
100	4" x 8"	used bricks	base
8	8'	2 x 4 #2 fir	posts
14	8'	2 x 2 #2 cedar	lattice frames
4	10'	2 x 4 #2 cedar	top plates
2	4' x 8'	¾" exterior plywood	roof
1	8'	¾" x ¾" quarter-round molding	roof
2	8'	1⅜" diameter wooden pole	roof
2	4' x 8'	diagonal cedar lattice	walls
1	4' x 8'	perpendicular cedar lattice	gables
12	8'	1 x 4 #2 pine	door and corner trim
1	10'	1 x 4 #2 pine	frieze board
1	10'	⅞" x 1⅛" nose and cove molding	gables
2	8'	1¹¹⁄₁₆" x 1⅜" solid crown molding	gables
2	12'	2 x 2 #2 cedar	gable lattice frame
1 sheet	4' x 4'	¾" exterior plywood (marine-grade)	brackets
1	6' x 9'	12 oz. canvas cloth, light green	
1 lb.	3d	galvanized common nails	
1 lb.	4d	galvanized finishing nails	
1 lb.	8d	galvanized finishing nails	
1 lb.	16d	galvanized common nails	
4	40d	galvanized finishing nails	
1 lb.	2½"	galvanized deck screws	
1 box	½"	staples	
8	40d	galvanized common nails	
8	¼" x 4"	galvanized lag screws	
½ cu. yd.		builder's sand	
1 jar		contact cement	
1 can		semi-gloss enamel paint	

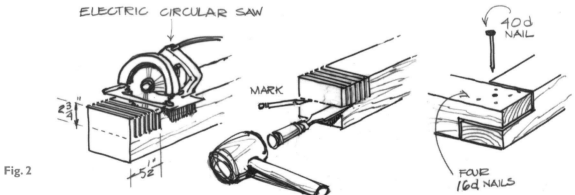

Fig. 2

ELECTRIC CIRCULAR SAW

2¾"

5½"

MARK

40d NAIL

FOUR 16d NAILS

Base

1. Begin by leveling a 5' × 5' area and removing any large roots or rocks. Cut the 6 × 6 pressure-treated (P.T.) timbers into four 5' lengths. To join the four beams at the corners, cut lap joints as follows (see **fig. 2**).

2. Adjust the saw blade so that it cuts halfway (2¾") through the beam. Starting at one end and continuing for 5½", make several cuts across the beam. Do the same for each beam end. Then, with a chisel and mallet, chop out the cut material to form an L-shaped notch.

3. Place the beams on the level site you have prepared, so that their ends overlap each other and form a 5' square. Check the diagonal distances between the corners, both of which should be 84¾". Drive a 40d nail into each corner and check the diagonals again. Then, drive four 16d nails into each corner joint to hold it in place (see **figs. 2 and 3**).

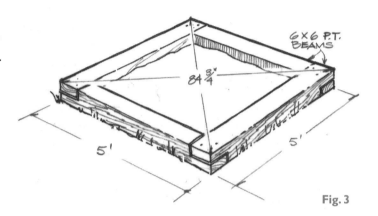

Fig. 3

Floor

Fill the squared frame with sand to 2" from the top. Compress the sand as much as possible by packing it down with your feet. Use a straight-edge to level off the top, and sprinkle the sand with water before laying the bricks. To keep the rows of bricks straight, measure the width of one brick and mark two parallel beams with this measurement. Continue doing this for each row. Place a nail at each mark, and connect the two nails with a string. Use this as your guide for laying the bricks. Stagger them as you go; where necessary, use bricks that you have broken in half with a brick chisel and hammer (see **fig. 4**).

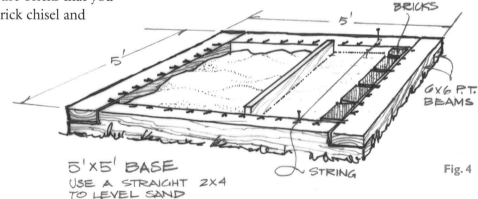

Fig. 4

Fig. 5

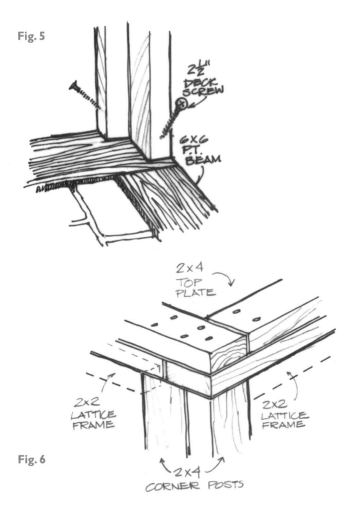

Fig. 6

Walls

1. Cut each 8' fir 2 × 4 into two 4' lengths. Use two lengths for each corner and one length to frame each side of the entrance. To form the corner posts, screw two 2 × 4s together in an L shape. Stand one post up in the corner and screw it to the 6 × 6 P.T. base, using 2½" deck screws (see **fig. 5**). Follow the same steps for the remaining three posts.

2. To stabilize the corner posts, construct a double top plate by screwing 2 × 4s to the tops of the corner posts with 2½" deck screws. Overlap the corners, and screw the 2 × 4s together (see **fig. 6**).

3. To build the lattice, install the outer vertical lattice frames at the entrances, followed by the horizontal frames, the lattice itself, and the inner frames. Use 8d nails for the frames and 3d nails for the lattice (see **figs. 1, 7a, 7b, and 7c**).

Roof

1. Cut two 38" × 72" pieces of ¾" plywood. Lay one piece on top of the wall frame, and use 4d nails to temporarily fasten the bottom edge of the roof panel to the top outside edge of the 2 × 4 wall framing. Make sure the short sides of

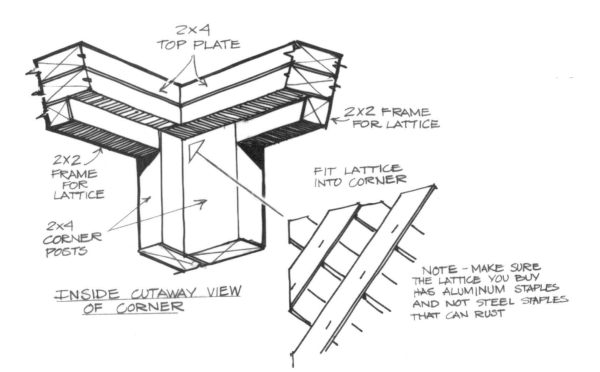

Fig. 7a

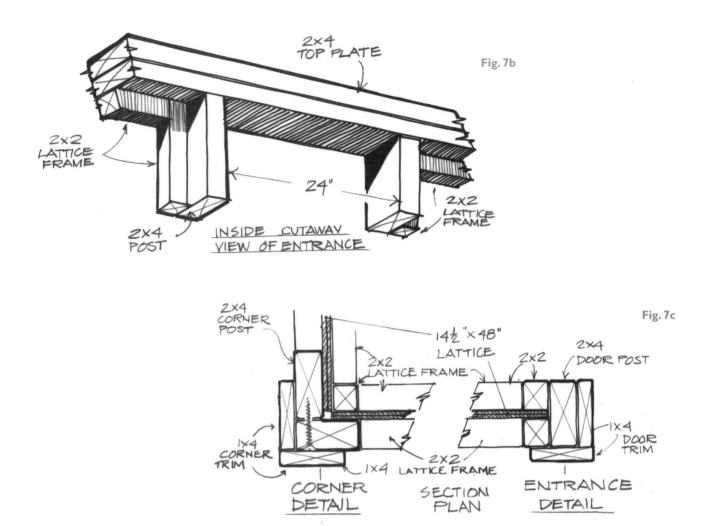

2×4
TOP PLATE

Fig. 7b

2×2
LATTICE
FRAME

24"

2×2
LATTICE
FRAME

2×4
POST

INSIDE CUTAWAY
VIEW OF ENTRANCE

2×4
CORNER
POST

Fig. 7c

14½"×48"
LATTICE

2×2
LATTICE FRAME

2×2

2×4
DOOR POST

1×4
CORNER
TRIM

1×4 LATTICE FRAME

2×2 LATTICE FRAME

1×4
DOOR
TRIM

CORNER
DETAIL

SECTION
PLAN

ENTRANCE
DETAIL

the plywood overlap the frame by 6". Repeat
this step with the second roof panel (see **fig. 8**).

2. To make the roof assembly process easier
and to protect the canvas from chafing later on,
use construction adhesive and 8d finishing nails
to glue and nail a 6' strip of quarter-round
molding to the top edge of one of the roof
panels (see **fig. 9**).

3. Standing inside the structure, and with
the help of an assistant, push the panels up

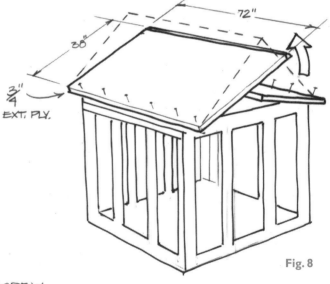

72"

30"

¾"
EXT. PLY.

Fig. 8

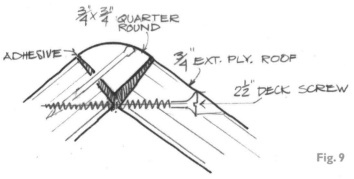

¾"×¾" QUARTER
ROUND

ADHESIVE

¾" EXT. PLY. ROOF

2½" DECK SCREW

Fig. 9

Fig. 10

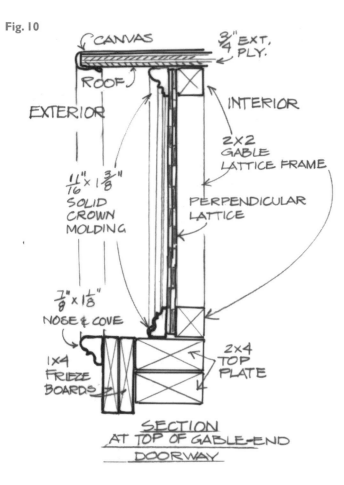

CANVAS

3/4" EXT. PLY.

ROOF

EXTERIOR

INTERIOR

2×2 GABLE LATTICE FRAME

$\frac{11}{16}" \times 1\frac{3}{8}"$ SOLID CROWN MOLDING

PERPENDICULAR LATTICE

$\frac{7}{8}" \times 1\frac{1}{8}"$ NOSE & COVE

1×4 FRIEZE BOARDS

2×4 TOP PLATE

SECTION AT TOP OF GABLE-END DOORWAY

Fig. 11

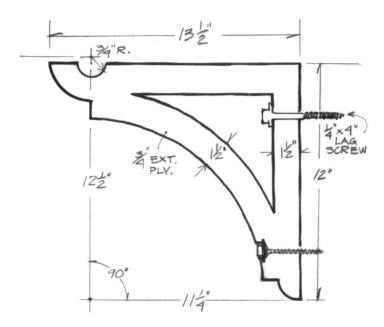

$13\frac{1}{2}"$

3/4" R.

3/4" EXT. PLY.

$1\frac{1}{2}"$

$1\frac{1}{2}"$

$\frac{1}{4}" \times 4"$ LAG SCREW

$12\frac{1}{2}"$

12"

90°

$11\frac{1}{4}"$

from the center until they meet at the top. (The temporary nails will bend and act as hinges.) Screw the bottom edges of the roof panels to the top plates with 2½" deck screws, and remove the temporary nails.

4. Standing on a ladder outside the playhouse, screw together the two top edges of the roof panels with 2½" deck screws. Make sure the screw heads are embedded in the surface of the plywood.

5. Apply contact cement to the roof, and then cover the roof with canvas cloth. Leave an overhang of 1½" on each side. Next, apply contact cement to the circumference of the roof poles. Staple the overhanging canvas onto 75"-long poles; turn the poles to wrap the canvas around them.

Gable and Door Trim

Trim the edges of the triangular gable with solid crown molding. Nail two 1 × 4 frieze boards to the edge of the top plates using 8d finishing nails. Nail the nose and cove molding to the top of the board faces using 4d finishing nails. Install the 2 × 2 gable lattice frame. Cut the perpendicular lattice to fit inside the frame, and secure it with solid crown molding (see **fig. 10**). Trim the other gable in the same way. Then, trim the corners and the four doorways with 4'-long 1 × 4 boards (see **fig. 1**).

Brackets

To hold the roof pole, use a jig saw to cut four brackets out of ¾" plywood, as shown in **fig. 11**. Screw them onto the corner post trim, using ¼" × 4" lag screws.

Paint

Paint the playhouse white throughout. It is easiest to paint everything after the playhouse has been assembled.

Summerhouse

A summerhouse situated at the edge of a garden, perhaps coming into sight after a turn in a garden path, can provide a secret retreat and refuge where one can read, write, or enjoy a few moments of solitude away from gardening and its endless tasks. This summerhouse is composed of eight combination screen and storm doors arranged in an octagon. The roof is made up of 1 × 4 lath boards spaced wide enough apart to allow sunlight to gently filter through without flooding the interior. All the doors are screened, allowing 360° of cross ventilation on hot summer days. In the spring and fall, when the weather is cool, the screens can quickly and easily be removed and replaced with storm windows. If possible, run an underground electric line from your house and install lights on the summerhouse, making it sparkle like a jewel box at night. For the ultimate effect, dig a shallow moat to reflect the summerhouse all year long.

Qty.	Size	Description	Location or Use
Octagonal Deck			
8	8'	4 × 4 P.T. lumber or cedar	deck posts
8	12'	2 × 6 P.T. lumber or cedar	deck joists
4	12'	2 × 8 P.T. lumber or cedar	floor joists
35	10'	2 × 6 T&G, V-groove	deck and floor
Summerhouse			
8	7'	4 × 4 cedar posts	wall corners
8	10'	2 × 4 #2 fir	top plates
32	7'	2 × 4 #2 fir	door-rough framing
8	7'	2 × 6 #2 fir	rafters
4	4 × 8	¼" clear Plexiglas	skylight
8	7'	2 × 2 cedar	skylight-triangular strips
8	7'	2 × 2 alum. edge flashing	skylight
1	18"	4 × 4 clear cedar	roof-center post
1	4 × 4	½" exterior plywood	roof cap
1	9'	24" copper flashing	roof cap
16	7'	1 × 6 #2 pine	doorjambs
16	38"	1 × 6 #2 pine	door headers
16	7'	1 × 8 #2 pine	exterior trim
16	7'	1 × 6 #2 pine	int. trim
16	7'	1 × 4 #2 pine	exterior trim
8	7'	1 × 3 #2 pine	interior block
32	7'	½ × 1⅝" casing	trim
3	½"	exterior plywood	soffits
3	¾"	exterior plywood	roof extension
8	3' × 6'8"	combination storm/screen French doors	walls
1	lock set	entry type with key	front door
4	1⅛" × 3"	brass hinges	doors
8		decorative wall brackets	doors
	240 lin. ft.	1 × 4 #2 pine	roof slats
1	35'	³⁄₁₆" stainless steel cable	rafters

Layout

Although not essential, this summerhouse looks best surrounded by an octagonal deck. This gives it the illusion of being situated on a pedestal and creates a gradual transition from the ground to the structure.

1. Clear an area 24' in diameter and establish a center point for a 19'-diameter circle, driving a ½" iron pipe in the ground.

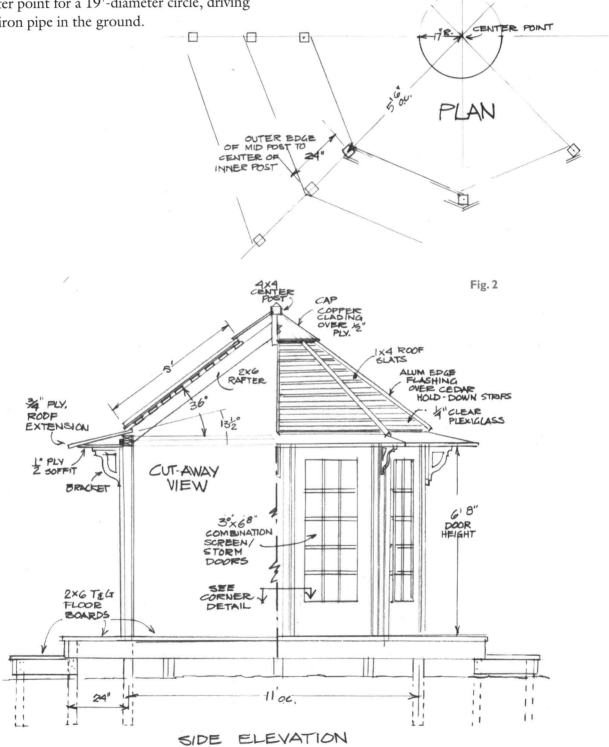

Fig. 1

CENTER POINT

1'8"

PLAN

5'6" O.C.

OUTER EDGE OF MID POST TO CENTER OF INNER POST

24"

Fig. 2

4×4 CENTER POST

CAP

COPPER CLADING OVER ½" PLY.

1×4 ROOF SLATS

ALUM EDGE FLASHING OVER CEDAR HOLD-DOWN STRIPS

¼" CLEAR PLEXIGLASS

5'

2×6 RAFTER

36°

13½°

¾" PLY. ROOF EXTENSION

½" PLY. SOFFIT

BRACKET

CUT-AWAY VIEW

3°×6'8" COMBINATION SCREEN/ STORM DOORS

6'8" DOOR HEIGHT

2×6 T&G FLOOR BOARDS

SEE CORNER DETAIL

24"

11' O.C.

SIDE ELEVATION

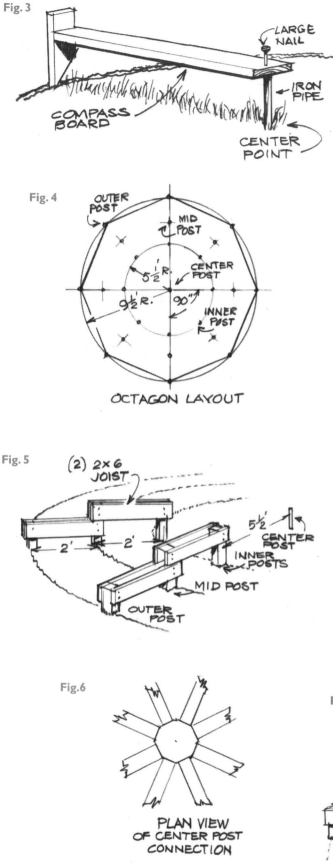

Fig. 3

LARGE NAIL

IRON PIPE

COMPASS BOARD

CENTER POINT

Fig. 4

OUTER POST

MID POST

CENTER POST

5½ R.

9½ R.

90"

INNER POST

OCTAGON LAYOUT

Fig. 5

(2) 2×6 JOIST

2'

2'

5½'

CENTER POST

INNER POSTS

MID POST

OUTER POST

Fig.6

PLAN VIEW OF CENTER POST CONNECTION

2. Make a compass out of a scrap 10'-long board by driving a heavy nail into one end and nailing a pointed stick into the other end. Use the stick end to scribe two circles on the ground — one with a 9½' radius and a smaller, inner circle with a 5½' radius. Scribe a line through the centers of the circles and scribe another line at right angles to the first line. Bisect the four resulting quadrants, creating eight points, equidistant apart, around the circumference of both circles. Mark all the points with wooden pegs or 12"-long lengths of rebar (see **figs. 3 and 4**).

Floor Framing

1. Dig 30"-deep holes directly over the inner circle points, and bury the ends of the 48"-long 4 × 4 P.T. posts in the ground. Do not backfill until you are sure they are equidistant apart (approximately 50" on-center). Dig another set of holes 2' out from the first set, and bury eight 48"-long 4 × 4 P.T. (middle) posts in the ground. Dig a third set of holes 2' out from the last set, and bury eight more 4 × 4 posts in the ground (to support the deck). Connect the middle and outer posts with 2 × 6 joists screwed to both sides of each post (see **fig. 5**).

2. To provide support for the floor of the summerhouse, make an octagonal center post by using a table saw to cut 1½" off each corner of the post, at a 45° angle (see **fig. 6**). Bury this center support post so that the top is level with the inner and middle posts. Attach 2 × 8 joist hangers to the inner posts. Nail the 2 × 8 joists radially from the center post to the inner posts (see **fig. 7**).

Fig.7

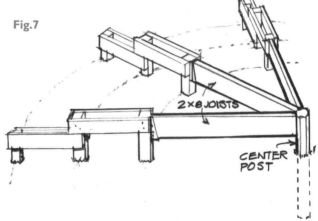

2×8 JOISTS

CENTER POST

3. Cut 2 × 6 T&G floor boards at approximately 67° angles at the ends, and nail them to the 2 × 8 floor joists in concentric circles. If your T&G floor boards have a V-groove on one side, you may want to place the groove side up, creating a pattern on the floor.

Wall Framing

1. To frame the summerhouse, begin by erecting eight 4 × 4 corner posts, each 6'9" long. Connect the posts at the top with two layers of 2 × 4s (top plates) screwed to the tops of the posts (see **fig. 8**). Locate the center between each pair of posts, then make a mark 19" in both directions. The space between these marks allows for the 36" wide doors, ¾" for each door jamb, and ¼" to shim each jamb. Screw a 2 × 4 stud to the floor and to the top plates just outside the marks. To make the frames for the doors, rip ½" off the 1 × 6 boards so that the boards are 5" wide, and use them to build eight U-shaped (upside down) door frames (see **fig. 9**).

2. Pre-cut door frames (jambs and headers) are often sold at lumber yards. Place the door frames in the doorways. Using one of the doors as a spacer, shim and screw the door frames to the studs. Allow a ³⁄₁₆" gap on all sides of the door to allow for expansion of the wood. Cut and nail a ⅜" × 1⅜" colonial doorstop for the door to rest against when it is closed (see **fig. 10**).

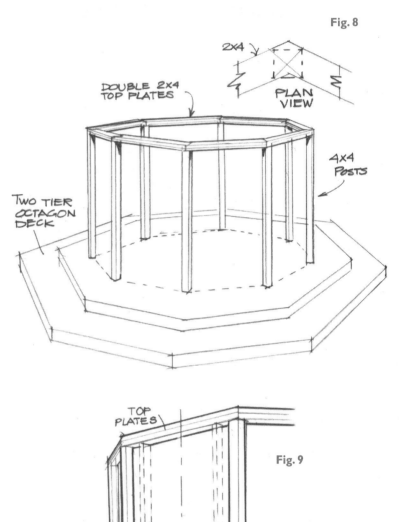

Fig. 8

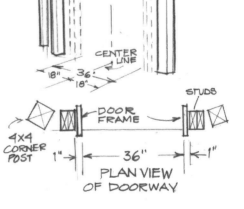

Fig. 9

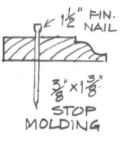

Fig. 10

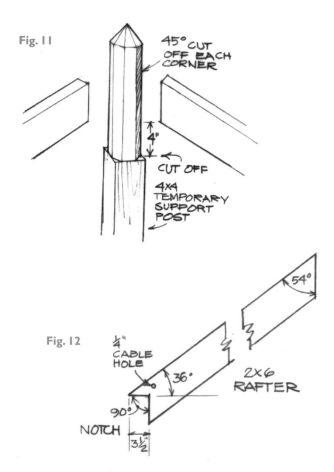

Fig. 11

45° CUT OFF EACH CORNER

4"

CUT OFF

4×4 TEMPORARY SUPPORT POST

Fig. 12

54°

¼" CABLE HOLE

36°

2×6 RAFTER

90°

NOTCH

3½"

Fig. 13

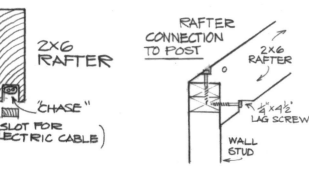

2×6 RAFTER

WOOD STRIP

"CHASE"

SLOT FOR ELECTRIC CABLE

Fig. 14

RAFTER CONNECTION TO POST

2×6 RAFTER

¼"×4½" LAG SCREW

WALL STUD

Rafters

To temporarily support the rafters at the top, install an 11'5" 4 × 4 post in the exact center of the summerhouse. Before setting up the post, cut 45° off each corner to make eight equal faces on the top end of the post where the rafters will meet (see **fig. 11**). To make the rafters, cut eight 2 × 6s, each 7' long. Cut a 54° angle at the top and a notch at the bottom of each rafter (see **fig. 12**).

Optional

1. Before installing the rafters, cut out a chase in the bottom of one of the rafters to provide a space to run an electric cable. The cut can be disguised by inserting a removable strip of wood trimmed to the exact dimension of the slot (see **fig. 13**).

2. Install one rafter at each corner post, using two ¼" × 4 ½" lag screws, installed at right angles to each other (see **fig. 14**).

Compression Cable

To keep the rafters from spreading under the weight of the roof, install a ³⁄₁₆"-diameter stainless steel cable through ¼" holes drilled near the bottom end of each rafter. Make a loop at each end of the cable and connect the two ends, using a turnbuckle and either cable clamps or a swaging sleeve. Tighten the cable by turning the turnbuckle (see **fig. 15**). After the cable is taut, cut off the center post 4" below the bottom edge of the rafters (see **fig. 11**).

Slats

To allow the sun to filter through the roof, install 1 × 4s horizontally, spaced 3½" apart (see

Fig. 15

³⁄₁₆" CABLE

SWAGING SLEEVE

TURNBUCKLE

CABLE CLAMPS

fig. 2). Use a scrap piece of 1 × 4 as a spacer. If you plan to paint the summerhouse, make sure that you paint both sides of the 1 × 4s before installing them.

Skylight

1. To keep out the rain, install a Plexiglas roof on top of the 1 × 4 slats. Two truncated pieces can be cut from one ¼"-thick 4 × 8 sheet of Plexiglas with a minimum of waste (see **fig.15**). Before taking this to the glass store, cut a scrap piece of ¼" thick plywood to size, and test fit it on all sides of the skylight to check that the dimensions haven't changed.

2. Plexiglas tends to expand and contract with changes in temperature. Therefore, it is necessary to drill (slowly) oversize screw holes (¼" diameter) to allow the Plexiglas some movement. In addition, the adjoining Plexiglas pieces should not butt together but should be spaced ½" apart. Fill the gap with clear Silicone caulk, held in place with a triangular piece of cedar, ripped to fit the angle where the two pieces of Plexiglas meet. Screw the triangular cedar strips to the top edge of the rafters, using 3" stainless steel screws (see **fig.16**).

3. To protect the triangular cedar strips from weathering, cover them with 2" × 2" aluminum edge flashing sold in most lumber yards (see **figs. 16 and 17**). Paint the aluminum flashing before you install it, and hold the pieces in place using construction adhesive.

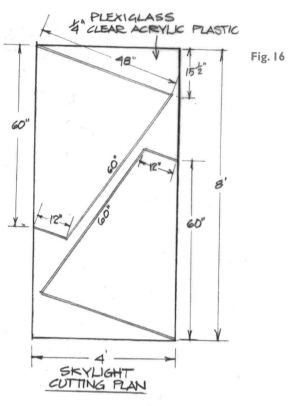

Fig. 16

SKYLIGHT CUTTING PLAN

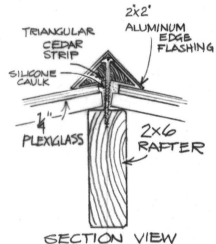

SECTION VIEW

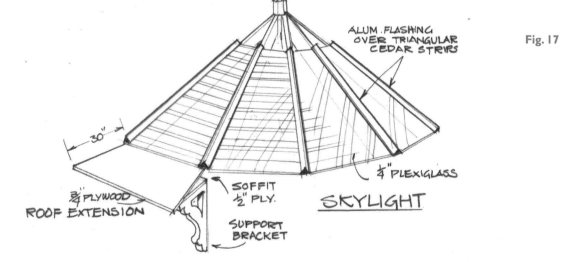

Fig. 17

SKYLIGHT

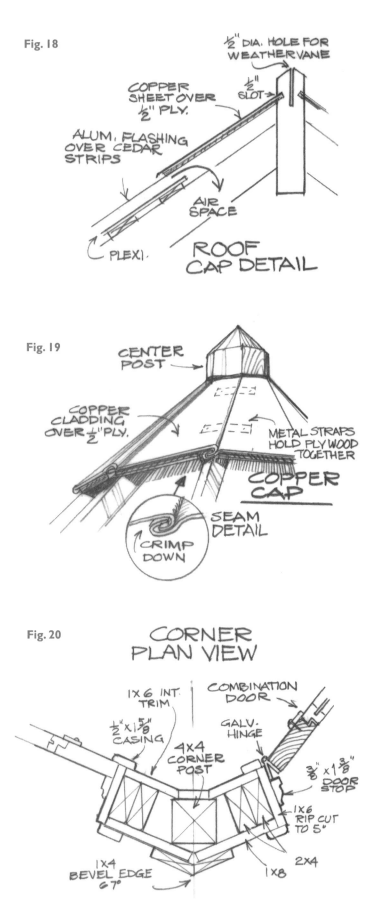

Fig. 18

½" DIA. HOLE FOR
WEATHERVANE

COPPER
SHEET OVER
½" PLY.

½"
SLOT

ALUM. FLASHING
OVER CEDAR
STRIPS

AIR
SPACE

PLEXI.

ROOF
CAP DETAIL

Fig. 19

CENTER
POST

COPPER
CLADDING
OVER ½" PLY.

METAL STRAPS
HOLD PLYWOOD
TOGETHER

COPPER
CAP

SEAM
DETAIL

CRIMP
DOWN

Fig. 20

CORNER
PLAN VIEW

1X6 INT.
TRIM

COMBINATION
DOOR

½" X 5⁄8"
CASING

GALV.
HINGE

4X4
CORNER
POST

3⁄8" X 1 3⁄8"
DOOR
STOP

1X6
RIP CUT
TO 5"

1X4
BEVEL EDGE
67°

2X4

1X8

Cap

Make the octagonal cap out of ½"-thick plywood pieces joined together by galvanized metal straps and fitted into a ½" slot in the top center post. The plywood lays on top of the triangular cedar strips and allows a 2" space for ventilation (see **figs. 18 and 19**). This space can be screened in if bugs are a problem. Cover the cap with copper bent over the plywood and joined at the seams (see **fig. 18**). Over time, this will weather to an aqua green. While you're working at the peak, bore a ½"-diameter hole, 9" deep, in the top of the center post to hold a weathervane.

Wall Corner Trim

Cut and nail 1 × 8s to the outside corners and 1 × 6s to the inside corners. Add ½" × 1⅝" trim (casing) to the interior and exterior of each doorway, and 1 × 4s to the outside corners. Add a filler block between the two 1 × 6s on the inside corners (see **fig. 20**).

Roof Extension

1. Cut eight truncated pieces of ¾" plywood, 30" deep, to fit under the bottom edge of the Plexiglas (see **fig. 17**). They should be deep enough so that there is no possibility that rain water will seep back into the interior of the summerhouse.

2. To support the plywood roof extensions, buy or build eight wall brackets and attach them to the beveled 1 × 4 corner trim boards. Build a ½"-ply soffit over the tops of the brackets to support the outside of the roof extensions (see **fig. 17**).

Doors

It's easier to paint the doors before you install them. Attach hinges and handles to the doors that will be operable, otherwise seal the doors, using caulking adhesive.

Shade Pavilion

If you have ever felt the thrill of walking through a house that was under construction and sensed the logic of the underlying structure, with its patterns of light filtering through the studs and joists, then you will like this shade pavilion. Designed to provide partial shade in sunny areas, it is built on sturdy 8' × 8' posts and can be constructed in one weekend.

Qty.	Size	Description	Location or Use
4	12'	8' × 8' P.T. posts	corner posts
6	10'	2 × 10 cedar or redwood	crosspieces
10	10'	2 × 6 cedar or redwood	rafters
12	8'	1 × 2 props	
4	80-lb. bags	concrete	
16	4"	½"-diameter galvanized lag screws	
2 lbs.	3½"	common galvanized nails	

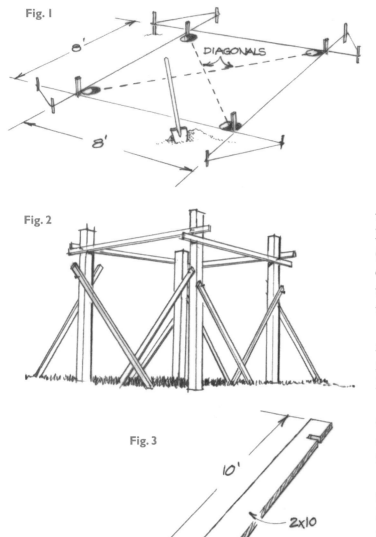

Fig. 1

DIAGONALS

8'

8'

Fig. 2

Fig. 3

10'

2x10

12"

1. Begin by leveling a flat area. Mark where the posts will go by setting four temporary stakes in an 8' × 8' square. Make sure that the stakes form a perfect square by measuring the diagonals — they should be of equal length (see Setting Corner Markers on page 10).

2. Using the temporary stakes as a guide, drive two additional stakes at each corner, 2' to 3' from each corner, and wrap a string around them as shown in **fig. 1**. Use these strings as a guide when digging the holes for the four corner posts. Dig each post hole at least 30" to 40" deep, and drop an 8 × 8 post (or a 12'-long used telephone phone) in each corner. Using 1 × 2 props, support the poles so they are plumb, but do not backfill until the top structure is in place (see **fig. 2**).

3. Check to make sure that the outside corners of the posts are 8' from each other, then nail temporary 1 × 2 crosspieces to the posts, to hold them in place (see **fig. 2**).

4. Trim four pieces of 2 × 10 to measure exactly 10' long. Measure 12" in from each end, and cut a 1½"-wide notch halfway through (see **fig. 3**).

5. Nail temporary blocks of scrap wood 7' up on the posts to support the 2 × 10 beams. Mark and drill two ⅜"-diameter pilot holes for the ½" × 4" lag screws (see **fig. 4**). Screw the beams to the posts, making sure the beam's notches fit together as shown in **fig. 5**.

6. Add an extra pair of 2 × 10s on the inside of the posts to carry the weight of the 2 × 6 rafters (see **fig. 6**).

7. Cut seven 2 × 6 rafters, each 10' long, and place them 12" apart across the top of the 2 × 10s. Toenail them in place, using 3½" galvanized common nails (see **fig. 7**).

8. Cut fourteen pieces of 2 × 6, each 24" long, and nail them 12" apart to the end 2 × 10 and at right angles to the two end rafters (see **fig. 8**).

9. Cut off the tops of the corner posts 12" above the tops of the rafters. Backfill the post holes with concrete, and wait several days before removing the 1 × 2 props.

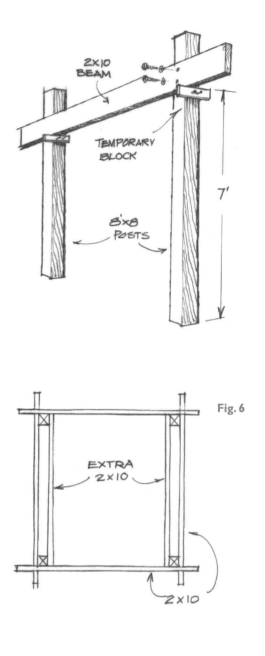

Fig. 4

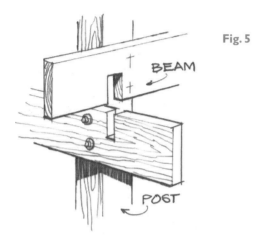

Fig. 5

Fig. 6

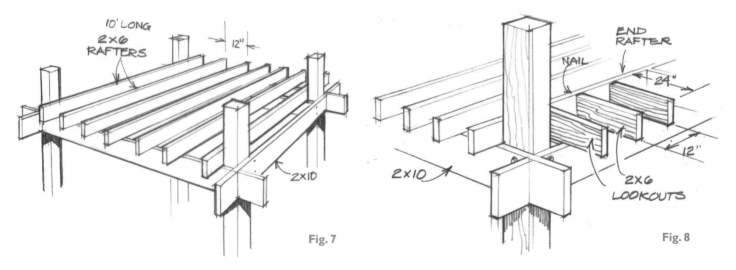

Fig. 7

Fig. 8

Fanciful Garden Kiosk

This decorative garden tool house serves as a convenient storage place for garden tools, close to where you will need them, while also providing an intriguing, fanciful focal point for your garden. It could be a perfect place to run a water line for flowers, and it could even feature a spigot and an elevated stand so you don't have to bend over when filling your watering can. As an optional feature, consider turning the top into a decorative birdhouse.

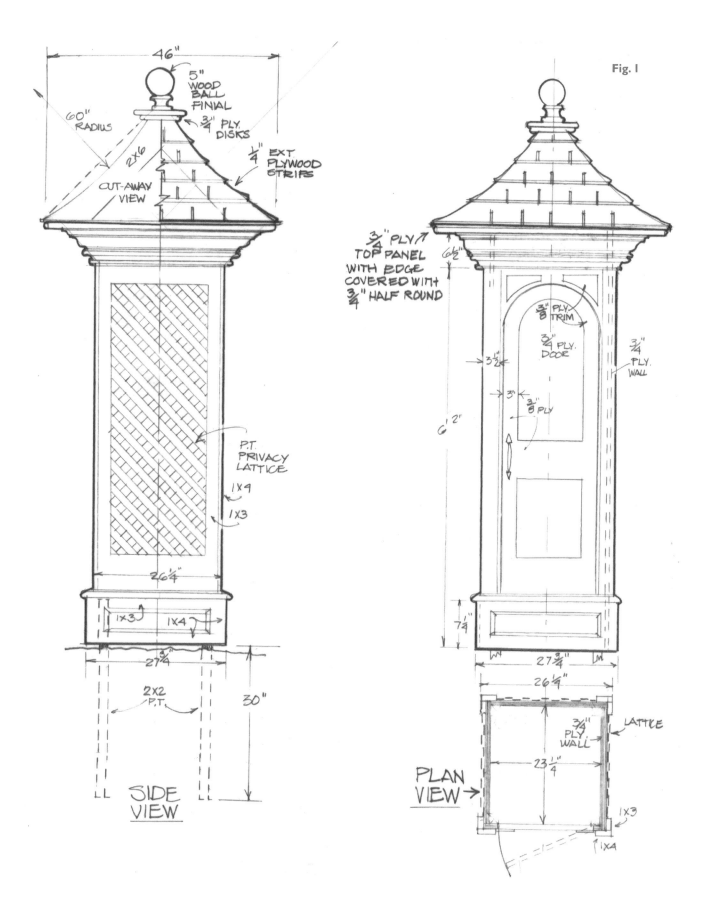

46"

5" WOOD BALL FINIAL

60" RADIUS

2×6

CUT-AWAY VIEW

¾" PLY. DISKS

¼" EXT PLYWOOD STRIPS

P.T. PRIVACY LATTICE

1×4

1×3

26¼"

1×3

1×4

27¾"

2×2 P.T.

30"

SIDE VIEW

Fig. 1

¾" PLY TOP PANEL WITH EDGE COVERED WITH ¾" HALF ROUND

6½"

⅜" PLY. TRIM

¾" PLY. DOOR

¾" PLY. WALL

3½"

3"

⅜" PLY

6'2"

7¼"

27¾"

26¼"

23¼"

¾" PLY. WALL

LATTICE

1×3

1×4

PLAN VIEW →

Qty.	Size	Description	Location or Use
2	4' × 8'	¾" exterior AC plywood	box and floor
1	4' × 8'	⅜" exterior AC plywood	door and trim
1	10'	1 × 8	base
1	10'	1 × 4	base trim
1	10'	1 × 3	base trim
1	8'	1¹⁄₁₆" × 1¹⁄₁₆" cove molding	base trim
1	8'	⅝" × 1⅝" bull nose	base trim
1	4' × 8'	⅛" privacy lattice	sides and back
1	12'	1 × 10 #2 pine	molding support
1	12'	1¹⁄₁₆" × 5¼" sprung crown molding	cornice molding
2	12'	⅜" × 1½" bull nose molding	cornice molding
1	12'	⁹⁄₁₆" × 2⅝" cove molding	cornice molding
1	16'	¾" half round molding	top panel edge
1	12'	2 × 6 #2 const. fir	rafters
1½ sheets	4' × 8'	¼" exterior AC plywood	roof
1	5"-diameter	wood finial ball	roof finial
1 bottle	8 oz.	Titebond II glue	
1 box	1"	galvanized wire nails	
3	1" × 3"	butt hinges	
1	5"	handle	
1 box	1½"	galvanized finishing nails	
1 qt.		exterior paint	
1 box	2"	galvanized finishing nails	

Sides

1. Begin by cutting two 4' × 8' sheets of ¾" exterior plywood in half lengthwise. Cut four pieces, each 80½" long. Glue and screw the four pieces together as shown in **fig. 2,** so that you end up with a 24¾" × 24¾"-square box.

2. To create the door, start by measuring in 3" from each side of the front. Draw a semi-circular 9⅜"-radius arc. Carefully cut out the door using an electric jig saw (see **fig. 3**).

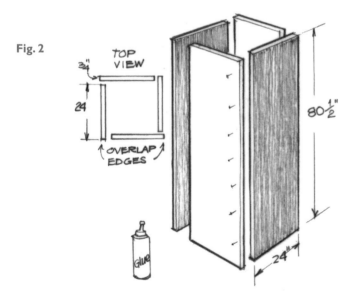

Fig. 2

Door Trim

Trace the door onto a piece of ⅜" exterior plywood, and mark the openings shown in **fig. 4.** Cut out the door trim, then glue and clamp it to the plywood door. Cut out the corner trim pieces from leftover ⅜" plywood (see **fig. 5**).

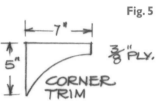

Fig. 3

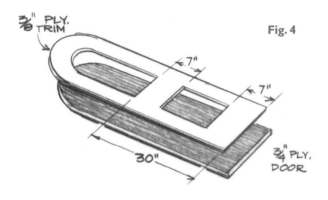

Fig. 4

Fig. 5

Floor

Cut a piece of ¾" plywood to the dimensions 23¼" × 23¼". Using scrap pieces of lumber for support, glue and screw the floor in place 7¼" up from the bottom of the box (see **fig. 6**).

Base Trim

Measure the outside perimeter of the base, and cut four 1 × 8 boards to fit around it. Glue and nail the four boards to the bottom. Cut pieces of 1 × 4 and 1 × 3 trim to frame the 1 × 8 boards, and glue in place. Cut four pieces of ¹¹⁄₁₆" × ¹¹⁄₁₆" cove molding to fit inside the 1 × 4 and 1 × 2 frames. Cut a ⅝" × 1⅝" bull nose stop to cover the top of the base and base trim. Miter the corners at 45°, and glue and nail in place using 1" galvanized wire nails and waterproof glue (see **fig. 7**).

Door

Hang the door on three 1" × 3" hinges, allowing a ⅛" gap on each side. Screw a 5" handle with a thumb latch onto the door (see **fig. 1**).

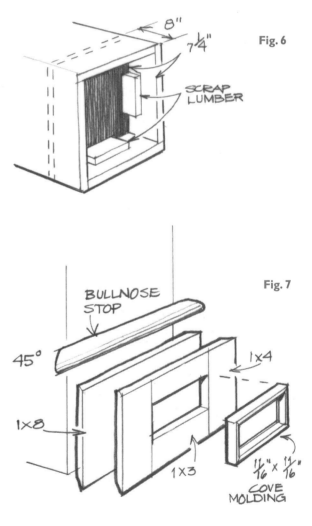

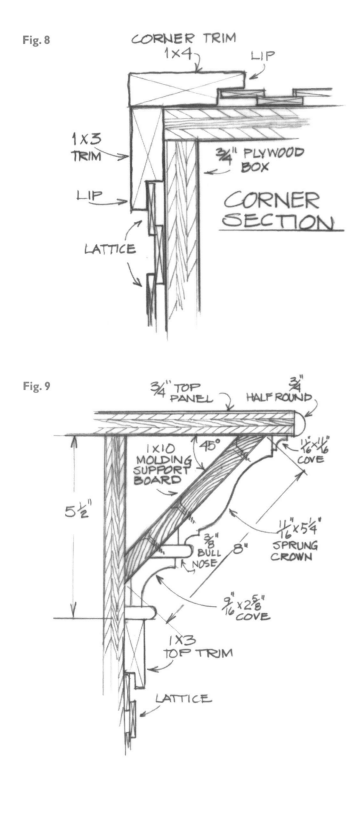

Fig. 8

CORNER TRIM
1×4

LIP

1×3 TRIM

LIP

LATTICE

¾" PLYWOOD BOX

CORNER SECTION

Fig. 9

¾" TOP PANEL

½ HALF ROUND

1×10 MOLDING SUPPORT BOARD

45°

5½"

3/8" BULL NOSE

8"

1¹⁄₁₆"×1¹⁄₁₆" COVE

1¹⁄₁₆"×5¼" SPRUNG CROWN

9⁄₁₆"×2⁵⁄₈" COVE

1×3 TOP TRIM

LATTICE

Back and Sides

1. Cover the corners of the box with a combination of 1 × 3s, 1 × 4s, and ⅛" lattice (see **figs. 1 and 8**). Make a ½" × ⅜" rabbet cut on the back of each piece to provide a lip to hold the lattice in place. Cut three pieces of ⅛" privacy lattice to cover the sides and back of the kiosk and fit inside the lip of the trim. Secure the lattice by attaching the trim pieces over it, using 2" galvanized finishing nails.

2. If you plan on painting this kiosk, paint the front and back of the lattice and the ¾" plywood sides before you nail them in place.

Molding Support

To provide a flat surface on which to attach the moldings, bevel cut an 8"-wide board, 45° on edge (see **figs. 9 and 10**). Make a compound miter cut at each end so that the boards will fit together at the corners. Cut a 46" square out of ¾" plywood, and screw it to the top of the box. Screw the molding support boards to the top panel and the box walls. Cut, glue, and nail ¾" half round molding to the edges of the top panel (see **fig. 9**).

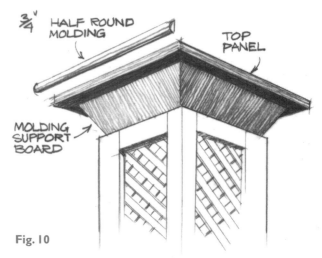

¾" HALF ROUND MOLDING

TOP PANEL

MOLDING SUPPORT BOARD

Fig. 10

Cornice Molding

To cut the various types of molding, make a simple cutting jig to guide your saw while making the cuts. Do this by joining together two 36"-long pieces of scrap 2 × 6. Screw a ¾"-square strip of wood to the front top surface to hold the bottom of the molding while you cut it. Reposition the strip to accommodate each different size of molding (see **fig. 11**). Using the miter box, cut and fit all the pieces of cornice molding (see **figs. 9 and 11**).

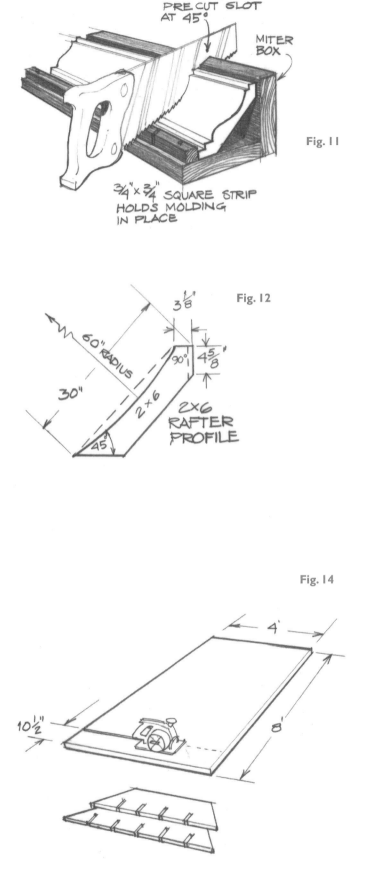

Fig. 11

Roof Rafters

Cut four pieces of 2 × 6 to a length of 30⅜". Draw a 60"-radius curve on one side of each piece, and cut out the pieces using an electric jig saw. Cut off the bottoms of the rafters at 45° angles, and cut the tops as shown in **fig. 12**. You will need to cut ¾" off two of the rafters in order to allow them to fit together at the center (see **fig. 13**).

Fig. 12

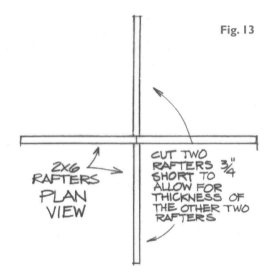

Fig. 13

Roof Shingles

From 1½ sheets of 4' × 8', ¼" exterior plywood, cut boards 10½" wide. Measure and cut each board to fit the rafters and to make five rows. Before attaching, kerf cut notches in the bottom edges to simulate shingles (see **fig. 14**). Using construction adhesive and 2" galvanized finishing nails, attach the boards to the rafters.

Fig. 14

Fig. 15

ROOF FINIAL

10" DISK

7" DISK

Finials

Cut two ¾" plywood disks, one 7" in diameter and the other 10" in diameter. Glue and screw them to the top of the rafters. Top off with a 5"-diameter wooden ball (see **fig. 15**).

Extras

1. As an added feature, you may want to attach a watering-can stand, providing a place to fill your watering can without bending over (see **fig. 16**). You may also want to build a rack on which to store your hose. Use the inside of your door to hold the most frequently used tools, such as clippers, spades, and loppers. Use the inside back wall to hang heavier tools, such as shovels, pick axes, and pitch forks.

2. To entice insect-eating birds to your garden, you can build a birdhouse in the roof by cutting an opening in the ¼" plywood shingles and custom fitting it to suit your needs (see **fig. 17**).

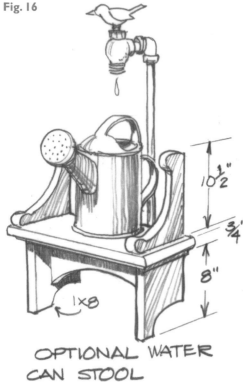

Fig. 16

10½"

¾"

8"

1x8

OPTIONAL WATER CAN STOOL

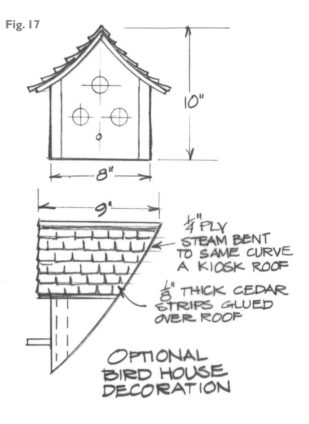

Fig. 17

10"

8"

9"

¼" PLY STEAM BENT TO SAME CURVE A KIOSK ROOF

⅛" THICK CEDAR STRIPS GLUED OVER ROOF

OPTIONAL BIRD HOUSE DECORATION

Rustic Cedar Gazebo

A gazebo deserves a perfect site — preferably one that overlooks a pond or lake, or has a view of the mountains with the sun rising or setting in the distance. Use it as a place to survey the seasons, somewhat protected from the elements yet surrounded by a 360° view. It is an ideal structure to use as an escape from the hectic pace of home and the workplace. If you are fortunate enough to live in a part of the country where cedar trees grow straight and tall, you should be able to find cedar posts for sale at your local nursery or landscape supply outlet at a reasonable price. In many regions, there are lumber companies that will let you know where you can find cedar logs sold directly from saw mills. To minimize the number of cedar logs needed, use stock lumber where it doesn't show, such as the floor and ceiling. Red and white cedar is wonderful to work with since it is so lightweight and easy to cut. It has the added advantage of being one of the most rot-resistant types of wood available and of having a pleasant, aromatic smell.

Fig. I

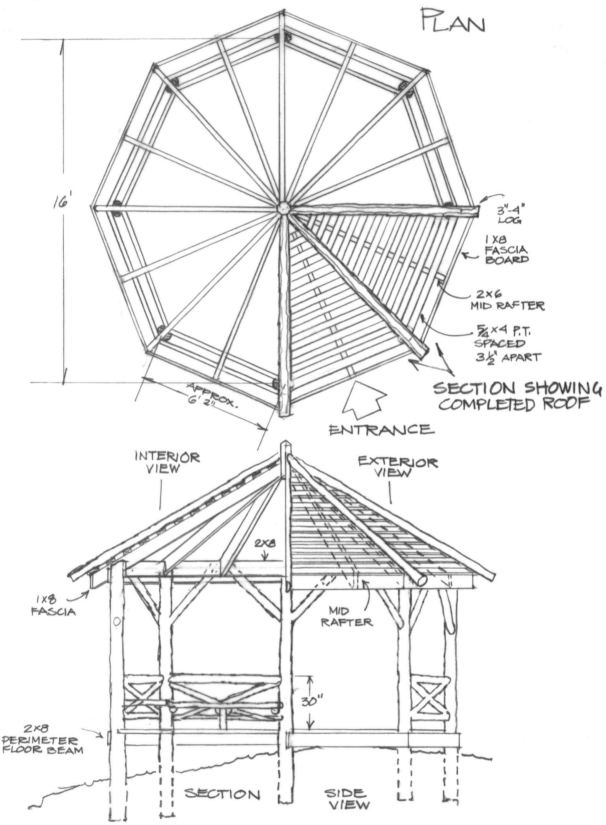

PLAN

16'

APPROX.
6' 2"

3"-4"
LOG

1 x 8
FASCIA
BOARD

2 x 6
MID RAFTER

5/4 x 4 P.T.
SPACED
3½" APART

SECTION SHOWING
COMPLETED ROOF

ENTRANCE

INTERIOR
VIEW

EXTERIOR
VIEW

2 x 8

MID
RAFTER

1 x 8
FASCIA

30"

2 x 8
PERIMETER
FLOOR BEAM

SECTION

SIDE
VIEW

Materials Needed

Qty.	Size	Description	Location or Use
8	10'6" min.	8"-diameter cedar post	perimeter
4	14'	2 × 8 fir	perimeter floor beams
1	6'	8' × 8' P.T. post	center post
8	8'	2 × 8 fir	floor joist
400 lin. ft.	2 × 6	P.T. lumber	flooring
8	14'	2 × 8 fir	top perimeter beams
16	12'	2 × 6 fir	rafters and mid-rafters
8	8'	1 × 8 cedar	fascias
200 lin. ft.	⁵⁄₄ × 4	P.T. boards	roof
8	12'	3"–4" logs	roof
1	12'	4 × 4 cedar post	roof
8	6'	4"-diameter cedar logs	railing
8	6'	3"-diameter cedar logs	bottom railing
16	6'	3"-diameter cedar logs	diagonals
48	6'	2"–3"-diameter cedar logs	seats
16	3'	cedar logs	knee braces
2	8'	2 × 2 P.T. stakes	batter posts
16	10'–16'	1 × 2 #2 pine	temporary braces
8	½" × 8"	eye bolts	posts
8	½" × 5"	lag screws	posts
1	gallon	wood preserve	posts
8	2 × 8	joist hangers	posts
32	½" × 5"	lag screws	braces
32	¼" × 4"	lag screws	braces
32	⅜" × 6"	lag screws	beams
2 lbs.	3½"	stainless steel screws	railings

Construction Comments

Much of the construction of this gazebo requires joining round logs together in what might seem like difficult joints. Actually, because of the nature of the rough wood, making joints is not that difficult. Quite often, an electric chain saw is the tool of choice. Just make sure to use both hands to hold the saw. Other tools you might consider are a portable electric grinder, a rotary rasp on an electric drill, a Lancelot, or the old reliable mallet and chisel (see **fig. 2**).

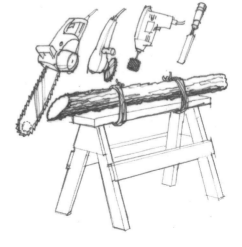

Fig. 2

Laying Out the Site

1. Clear an area 24' in diameter, and locate the center point. Scribe two circles in the ground — one with an 8' radius and a larger one with a 12' radius. To do this, drive a short post in the ground at the center point and drive a nail part way into the top. Use a sharp stick and a wire tied to the nail to scribe the circles (see **fig. 3**).

Fig. 3

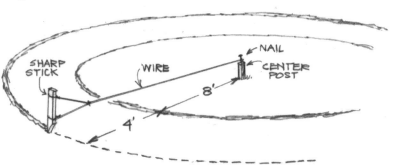

NAIL
CENTER POST
WIRE
SHARP STICK
CENTER POST
8'
4'

Fig. 4

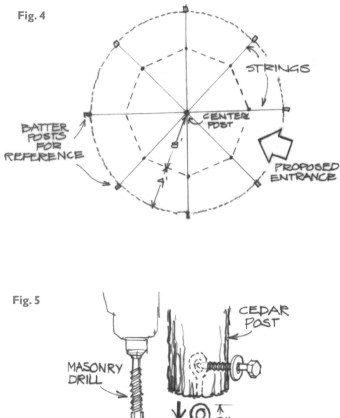

STRINGS
BATTER POSTS FOR REFERENCE
CENTER POST
PROPOSED ENTRANCE
8'
4'

2. Next, mark off eight points equidistant from each other on the outer circle. Plan the entrance to the gazebo now and make sure none of the eight points lie where the entrance will be located. Stretch a mason's line from each point across the center line to the opposite side to make sure they are positioned correctly, and hammer a small batter post at each point. The batter posts can be either 2 × 2 P.T. stakes or 24"-long reinforcing rods, driven 12" into the ground. Use these posts to help you relocate the position of the eight corner points along the inner circle in case they get lost while digging the holes for the corner posts (**see fig. 4**). Check to make sure the cross strings are level by using a mason's level, and mark the batter posts accordingly.

Excavation

Dig eight 16"-diameter holes at least 30" into the ground for the corner posts of the gazebo. If you hit bedrock, drill out a 6"-deep hole using a ½"-diameter masonry drill, and cement a ½" × 8" eye bolt into the hole. Bore a hole into the bottom of the cedar post large enough to accept the eye bolt. Drop the bottom end of the post over the eye bolt, and screw a ½"-diameter lag screw into the post and into the eye bolt (see **fig. 5**).

Fig. 5

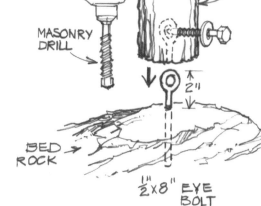

MASONRY DRILL
CEDAR POST
2"
BED ROCK
½"x8" EYE BOLT

Erecting the Posts

Cut eight 8"-diameter cedar posts, 10' 6" long, and bury the bottom 30" in the ground. If the ground is sloped, the posts will have to be cut longer so that the tops remain level (see **fig. 6**). Soak the butt ends of the posts in wood preserver, or paint them with roofing cement (tar). Stand the posts up in the holes, but do not backfill them until the structure is framed (allowing you to make adjustments if necessary). Nail 1 × 2 temporary braces to the posts to keep them perfectly plumb and uniformly spaced.

Floor

1. Make a mark 12" above ground on the post where the ground is highest. Stretch a level line to the opposite post and mark it. Continue around until all the posts are marked at the same level (see **fig. 6**).

2. Cut and screw 2 × 8 perimeter floor beams to the outside of the posts, beveling the ends 68° where they meet (see **fig. 7**).

3. To support the floor joists at the center, cut a center post out of either 8' × 8' P.T. lumber or a 12"-diameter locust post, and bury the bottom 30" below ground in concrete, exactly in the center of the structure. Bury it so that the top is 8¾" below the top of the intended finished floor. This allows 7¼" for the floor joists and 1½" for the flooring (see **fig. 8**).

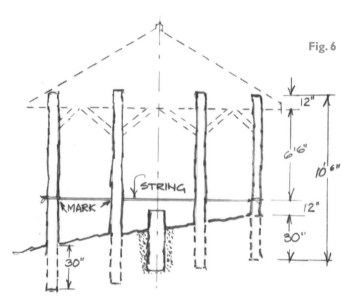

Fig. 6

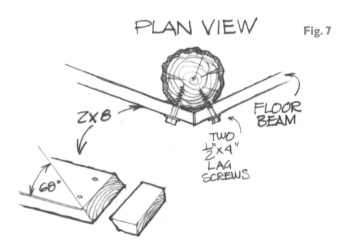

PLAN VIEW   Fig. 7

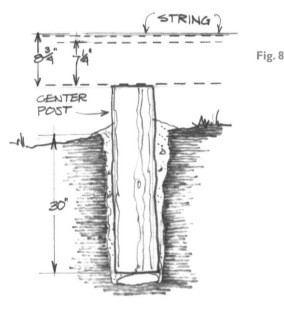

Fig. 8

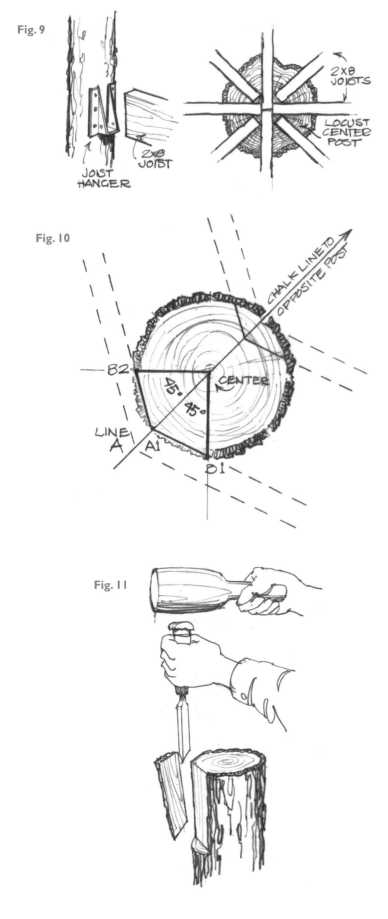

Fig. 9

4. Cut eight 2 × 8 joists to fit against the outside posts, with the other end resting on the center post. Attach the joists to the outside posts with metal joist hangers, and toenail them together at the center (see **fig. 9**).

5. The flooring is made up of 2 × 6 P.T. lumber, cut and laid in octagonal rows, leaving a 3⁄16" space between boards. Use a chop saw to miter the ends of each board at 6° angles.

Beams

1. To make the notches for the beams and the rafters, snap a chalk line across the tops of two opposite posts over their center points (see line A, **fig. 10**). Draw 45° angled lines on either side of the chalk line on the posts (see lines B1 and B2, **fig. 10**). Then draw lines from B1 and B2 to A1 (see **fig. 10**). This gives you the proper angles to notch the outside of the posts to support the outside beams.

2. Follow the same procedure for the inside beams. Cut out the notches using a chisel and mallet (see **fig. 11**). Following the chalk line as a guide, use an electric chain saw to cut a 1½"-wide notch in the top of the post to hold the rafters (see **fig. 12**). Cut off the tops of the posts at 30° angles to match the slope of the roof. Temporarily attach each pair of 2 × 8 beams by screwing them to the posts with two 3⁄8" × 6" lag screws. Bevel the end of each beam at a 68° angle, and allow room for the rafters by spacing them 1½" apart.

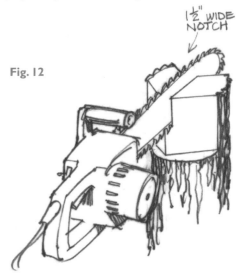

Fig. 12

Knee Braces

Attach a 3'-long knee brace to each side of each post by notching out a ½"-deep shoulder to accept each one. Screw the bottom end of each knee brace to the post, using ½" × 5" lag screws. Sandwich the opposite end of the brace between the two 2 × 8 beams, and secure with two ¼" × 4" lag screws (see **fig. 13**).

Rafters

1. Use 2 × 6 #2 construction lumber for the rafters. In order to support the rafters in the center of the gazebo, erect a temporary 4 × 4 post, supported by four temporary braces. Make the top of the post pointed by cutting it off at a 45° angle on all four sides. Make temporary supports for the rafters by nailing four pieces of scrap lumber to the posts (see **fig. 14**).

2. Make a 30° angled plumb cut at the top of each rafter. Since four of the rafters will be attached to the four corners of the center post, make a V-shaped cut in the end of each of these four rafters (see **fig. 15**). Let the bottom ends of all eight rafters fall into the slots provided in the ends of the eight posts. This will require unscrewing the 2 × 6 beams and screwing them together again. Allow the bottom ends of the rafters to extend well past the posts, and cut them off later (see **fig. 16**).

3. Install an additional 2 × 6 rafter midway between each pair of existing rafters. Cut both ends of the rafters off plumb, and toenail them to the beams and existing rafters.

4. Check to make sure that the posts remain plumb, as there will be a tendency for the rafters to push the posts during construction. To prevent this from happening, temporarily nail a 16' 1 × 2 from each post to its opposite post.

Roof

The roof is made up of ⁵⁄₄ × 4 P.T. boards, spaced 3 ½" apart to allow light to filter through the interior. Before attaching the boards, stain them a grayish brown to match the color of the cedar logs after they have weathered. Cover the rafter

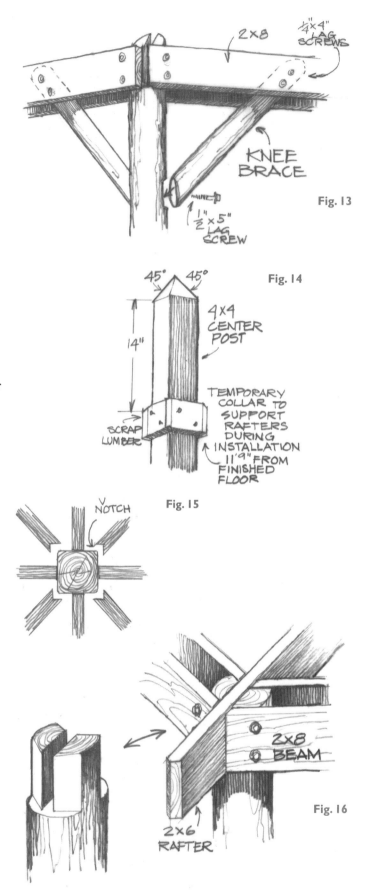

Fig. 13

Fig. 14

Fig. 15

Fig. 16

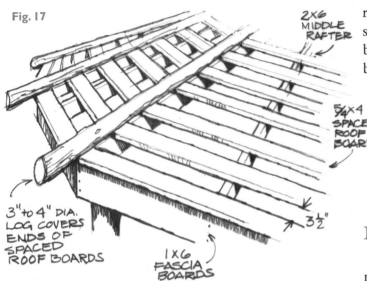

Fig. 17

2x6 MIDDLE RAFTER

5/4 X 4 SPACED ROOF BOARDS

3½"

3" to 4" DIA. LOG COVERS ENDS OF SPACED ROOF BOARDS

1 X 6 FASCIA BOARDS

ends by nailing 1 × 6 cedar fascia boards across them (see **fig. 17**). Cover the joints where the roof boards meet with 3" to 4"-diameter straight logs nailed to the corner rafters. It may be necessary to carve out a V-section along the bottom of the log to make it fit (see **fig. 18**).

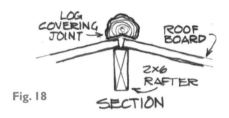

LOG COVERING JOINT

ROOF BOARD

2x6 RAFTER

Fig. 18

SECTION

Railings and Seating

1. The railings and seating section may take more time to build than the rest of the structure, however it is the most rewarding part, since this is what gives the rustic retreat the look that it deserves. Use only straight cedar logs, and do not remove the bark. Pre-drill all screw holes, and use stainless steel screws for longevity.

2. You can follow the simple design shown here for the railings or get creative and branch out, using curved pieces or crooked branches.

3. To make the pieces fit together, use a rotary rasp to carve out the rail to fit the outside curve of the post to which it will be joined (see **fig. 19**). Screw together all the joints, and test each one before moving to the next. Follow the dimensions shown in **fig. 20**.

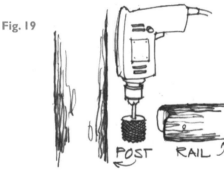

Fig. 19

POST   RAIL

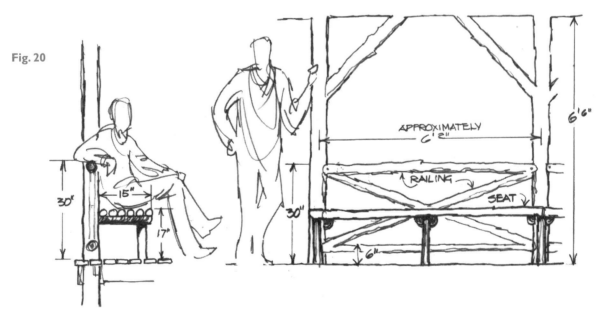

Fig. 20

30"

15"

17"

APPROXIMATELY 6' 2"

RAILING

SEAT

30"

6"

6' 6"

Recommended Further Reading

Books

Architectural Graphic Standards.
Charles G. Ramsey & Harold R. Sleeper. John Wiley & Sons Publishing Co., 1530 South Redwood Rd., Salt Lake City, Utah. 1970.
The Architect's Bible.

Building Small Barns, Sheds & Shelters. Monte Burch. Garden Way Publishing, Pownal, VT. 1983.
A practical guide to building barns and accessory buildings.

Building Thoreau's Cabin. Stephen Taylor. Pushcart Press, Wainscott, NY. 1992.
A philosophical description of one man's experience in building a small cabin (not Thoreau's!).

Handmade Houses. Art Boericke & Barry Shapiro. Scrimshaw Press, San Francisco, California. 1973.
Color photos of many owner built houses.

Playhouses You Can Build. David & Jeanie Stiles. A Firefly Book, Willowdale, Ontario, Canada. 1998.
Everything you need to know about building a playhouse — from a simple cardboard-box playhouse to an elaborate shingled house. Includes materials lists and detailed illustrations.

Rustic Retreats — A Build-It-Yourself Guide. David & Jeanie Stiles. Storey Books, Pownal, VT. 1998.
Illustrated, step-by-step instructions and basic building techniques for 20 outdoor structures including: a sauna hut, river raft, and yurt.

Sheds — The Do-It Yourself Guide for Backyard Builders. New — revised and expanded. David Stiles. A Firefly Book, Willowdale, Ontario, Canada. 1998.
Everything you need to know about building a shed, including materials lists, step-by-step illustrated instructions, and photographs.

Shelters, Shacks & Shanties. D. C. Beard. Charles Scribner's Sons, New York, NY. 1972.
The granddaddy of huts in America — an old book but worth re-reading.

Tree Houses — You Can Actually Build. David & Jeanie Stiles. Houghton Mifflin Publishing, Boston, MA. 1998.
The ultimate book on building your own tree house, including illustrations and photographs.

Woodcraft & Camping. Bernard S. Mason. Dover Publications, Inc., New York, NY. 1974.
A very good book on Indian lore, camping, and shelters.

Periodicals

Cottage Life
111 Queen Street
East Toronto, Ontario
M5C 1S2
416-360-6880
A magazine targeted toward lakeside living.

Heartland USA
174 Middlesex Turnpike
Burlington, MA 01803.
Information and articles on everything that has to do with the outdoors, from structures to sports.

Index

Other Storey Titles You Will Enjoy

Rustic Retreats: A Build-It-Yourself Guide, by David and Jeanie Stiles. Illustrated, step-by-step instructions for more than twenty low-cost, sturdy, beautiful outdoor structures. Projects include a water gazebo, sauna hut, triangular tree house, log cabin, and yurt. 160 pages. Paperback. ISBN 1-58017-035-8.

Build Your Own Low-Cost Log Home, by Roger Hard. Recognized as one of the best books on this popular subject, *Build Your Own Low-Cost Log Home* features both line drawings and photographs. The author offers pages of options to help you create beautiful and affordable log house designs. 208 pages. Paperback. ISBN 0-88266-399-2.

Landscaping Makes Cents: A Homeowner's Guide to Adding Value and Beauty to Your Property, by Frederick C. Campbell and Richard L. Dubé. Add substantial investment value and beauty to a home with this guide to landscape design. Explains how to create a landscape plan, determine a budget, choose a contractor, and achieve substantial financial return on a limited budget. 176 pages. Paperback. ISBN 0-88266-948-6.

Waterscaping: Plants and Ideas for Natural and Created Water Gardens, by Judy Glattstein. Packed with information on moist and wet spot gardening, installing pools, container water gardens, and border treatments. 192 pages. Paperback. ISBN 0-88266-606-1.

Building with Stone, by Charles McRaven. An introduction to the art and craft of creating stone structures, including finding stone, tools to use, and step-by-step instructions for projects such as walls, buttresses, fireplaces, a barbecue pit, a stone dam, and even a home or barn. Also includes instruction on proper restoration techniques for stone structures. 192 pages. Paperback. ISBN 0-88266-550-2.

Building Stone Walls, by John Vivian. A step-by-step guide to building both freestanding and retaining walls. Includes equipment requirements, instructions for creating wall foundations, coping with drainage problems, and hints for incorporating gates, fences, and stiles. 112 pages. Paperback. ISBN 0-88266-074-8.

Step-by-Step Outdoor Stonework, edited by Mike Lawrence. Over twenty easy-to-build projects for your patio and garden, including walls, arches, bird baths, sun dials, and fountains. Includes information on estimating costs, selecting tools and materials, and preparing the site. 96 pages. Paperback. ISBN 0-88266-891-9.

Stonescaping: A Guide to Using Stone in Your Garden, by Jan Whitner. A thorough guide to incorporating stone into many garden features, including paths, steps, walls, ponds, and rock gardens. More than 20 designs are included. 176 pages. Paperback. ISBN 0-88266-755-6.

These books and other Storey Books are available at your bookstore, farm store, garden center, or directly from Storey Publishing, Schoolhouse Road, Pownal, Vermont 05261, or by calling 1-800-441-5700. Or visit our website at www.storey.com

GREYSCALE

BIN TRAVELER FORM

Cut By _Cornelius Williams_ Qty _27_ Date _8-30-2024_

Scanned By _Nelly Torres_ Qty _27_ Date _08/30_

Scanned Batch IDs

_____ _666328431_ _____

Notes / Exception

_____

_____

_____

_____

_____